A+M
P

Fireside Book
OF
FOLK SONGS

Selected and edited by

Margaret Bradford Boni

Arranged for the piano by

Norman Lloyd

Illustrated by

Alice and Martin Provensen

Simon and Schuster

To My Sister
IRITA VAN DOREN

DESIGNED AND PRODUCED BY THE SANDPIPER PRESS AND ARTISTS AND WRITERS GUILD, INC. PUBLISHED BY SIMON AND SCHUSTER, INC., ROCKEFELLER CENTER, NEW YORK 20. PRINTED IN THE UNITED STATES OF AMERICA BY WESTERN PRINTING AND LITHOGRAPHING CO.

THIRD PRINTING

GENERAL ACKNOWLEDGMENTS

"Lili Marlene": by permission of the Attorney General in the public interest under License No. E-1206; copyright vested in the Attorney General, pursuant to law; English words used by permission of E. B. Marks Music Corp., N. Y. "Johnny Has Gone for a Soldier": by permission; copyright 1940 by John Allison, from John Allison Collection. "Who Can Retell?" and "Hanukkah Song" from *The Gateway to Jewish Song* by Judith Eisenstein, and "Glee Reigns in Galilee" from *Songs of Zion* by Harry Coopersmith, by permission Behrman House, Inc., publishers, N. Y. "Arkansas Traveler": words by David Stevens; by permission C. C. Birchard and Co. "Jeannette, Isabella": words by Berta Elsmith; by permission C. C. Birchard and Co. "Day Is Dying in the West": by permission Chautauqua Institution and Novello, Ltd. "Au Clair de la Lune": words by C. F. Manney from *The Junior A Cappella Chorus Book* published and copyrighted by Oliver Ditson Co. "Marche Lorraine": by permission of Enoch & Cie., Editeurs de Musique, Paris. "Waltzing Matilda": by permission; copyright 1936 by Allan & Co., Prop. Ltd., Melbourne; copyright 1941 by Carl Fischer, Inc., N. Y.; international copyright secured. "Rise Up, Shepherd, an' Foller": from *Religious Folk Songs of the Negro,* ed. by R. Nathaniel Dett, Hampton Institute Press. "The Lonesome Road": by permission, from Dorothy Scarborough, *On the Trail of the Negro Folk Song,* Cambridge, Harvard Univ. Press, 1925. "La Jesucita": by courtesy José Limon. "Peter Gray": by permission John A. Lomax. "Meadowlands," "Moscow," and "Tachanka": copyright E. B. Marks Music Corp. "Los Cuatro Generales," "Freiheit," and "The Peat-Bog Soldiers": copyright 1943 by Music Products, Inc., and Keynote Recordings, Inc.; by permission. "Every Night When the Sun Goes In": from *English Folk Songs from the Southern Appalachians,* coll. by Cecil Sharp, ed. by Maud Karpeles, by permission Oxford Univ. Press, London (Carl Fischer, Inc., N. Y., American agents). "The Coasts of High Barbary": copyright 1933 by Paull-Pioneer Music Corp., N. Y.; used by permission from the book *Keep on Singing.* "El Cuando": from *Los Origines del Arte Musical en Chile* by Eugenio Pereira Salas, Univ. de Chile, Santiago, 1941; translation by John W. Beattie. "The Young Voyageur": music by permission G. Schirmer, Inc., N. Y. "Robin M'aime": copyright 1928 by G. Schirmer, Inc.; by permission. "Careless Love": by permission Elie Siegmeister. "La Vidalita": from *Canciones Tipicas,* copyright 1941 by Irma Labastille, by special permission of author and publishers, Silver Burdett Co., N. Y. "Sit Down, Sister": from *Sing Me Your Song, O!* by Janet E. Tobitt. "John Henry": words from Guy B. Johnson, *John Henry: Tracking Down a Negro Legend,* Univ. of North Carolina Press, Chapel Hill, N. C.; by permission. "Now Let Me Fly": from *Rolling Along in Song* by J. Rosamond Johnson, copyright 1937 by The Viking Press, Inc., N. Y.

Appreciation is expressed particularly to Gladys Chamberlain of the Music Library, 121 East 58th Street, New York City, for invaluable assistance in the preparation of songs for this book.

Preface

THERE IS SOMETHING about the haunting melodies and the simple but inimitable verses of peasants and spinners, of fishermen, sailors and rude soldiery, which has perennial appeal to their descendants and those who have come to share their inheritance. Whether it be "Eileen Aroon," "Shenandoah," "Auprès de ma blonde," "Santa Lucia," or any of a thousand others, each generation that hears them for the first time is stirred again; and those who have retired to the chimney corner are moved by poignant memories.

The Fireside Book of Folk Songs may stimulate interest in our cultural history and in so doing it will do well, but its primary purpose, as the title implies, is to encourage the domestic performance of the songs of long ago that are still the songs of today.

It is characteristic of the songs of the people that they call for group performance. Many of them—work songs, dance songs, nursery rhymes, songs of festival —were so rendered from their inception; but even those conceived as solos have by their familiarity invited companionable unison whenever two or three or more people are gathered together. The custom is as old as the hills and as indestructible. Our familiar word "vaudeville" comes from the genial practice of groups of musical versifiers who gathered together for singing—and drinking—purposes in the French *Vau de Vire* in the early 14th century. In secular circles the custom was hoary then, as was congregational singing in the churches.

It is with a view to this pleasant custom that the arrangements of the tunes have been made. To avoid the monotony and vulgarity, no attempt has been made to persuade one style of accompaniment to suit varying styles of melody, and the square-toed "oom-pah" bass has been studiously avoided. A straight four-part harmonization has been used for songs likely to be sung in this way; and where the song seemed to offer a great deal of freedom in interpretation, the inherent possibilities of the tune have been exploited in the accompaniment. Phrasing, dynamic marks, pedalling and even fingering have been indicated where they appeared necessary to the full realization of the musical setting.

I wish to acknowledge my indebtedness to Anne Brooks for writing the introductions to the five sections, and so skillfully revealing the basic feeling which guided my choice of songs.

Here then is a collection of some of the best-loved songs in the world, as they have made their appearance on the American scene or become for the most part duly naturalized. They are filled with pathos, humor, struggle, whimsicality, tragedy and boisterous comedy which are the ingredients of our common lot. They are good to sing, better if sung with others, and best of all if sung again.

MARGARET BRADFORD BONI

Table of Contents

BALLADS AND OLD FAVORITES

Ballads and Old Favorites

THE BALLAD, or folk song, is the world's first newspaper and informal history book. It came into being as a sort of tabloid record of battles, adventures, and scandals in the days when an illiterate community depended for its news on the minstrels who roamed the countryside. And the form of the folk song served a practical purpose. The minstrel, having much news to report, could not rely entirely on his memory. A ballad stanza by its rhyme scheme and general circumscribed framework helped him to supply details which might otherwise be forgotten—to give accurate versions of names and times and places, and to recall the sequence of an event as it really happened.

After its first performance the ballad grew by itself, taking on a character of its own. A song which caught a community's fancy was repeated, and since it was learned aurally it was generally repeated inaccurately. The local songsters added improvements to it—tricks of phrasing which were not in the original work, additions of verses as events took place or were forgotten, and rhythmical changes as new wordings demanded new accent stresses. Only the best elements in the songs continued. Only the best of the ornamentations or changes were popular. And through centuries of weeding out, many of the ballads have come to be extremely subtle and delicate works—probably bearing little resemblance to their first crude versions. In fact, the taste and sensitive craftsmanship of some of the earlier folk songs is so highly regarded by professional musicians that many of the greatest and most elaborate orchestral and operatic works contain as their theme the simple, lovely threads of a nation's ballads.

The art of ballad singing took on a definite form too. At large community gatherings where a popular ballad was sung, it was as much a dance as a song. In fact, some etymologists maintain that the two words "ballad" and "ballet" spring from the same root and at one time were indistinguishable. This meant that the minstrel or a "leader" sang the verse and the community at large joined in on an answering chorus—almost a dramatic dialogue in music. It is interesting that these forms have died out or been maintained according to the nature of the community. In England and in western Europe where agricultural work has become an individual affair, the large choruses are no longer practical and the songs of the people have become solos and individual ballads. In the Balkans, Russia, and Africa, and on our own plantations of the South, where work is still communal, the folk song keeps its choral form and serves as an incentive to work rather than as a spare-time entertainment.

A nation's characteristics dictated other differences in the music too. The folk songs of various lands have their own styles and traditions, so that they are readily recognizable as national products. The simplicity of an English ballad bears little resemblance to the elaborately ornamented Spanish song. The Dutch or German song is solid and hearty. The American ballad has great liveliness and vigor. In fact, it is in the American ballad, with—in so many cases—its European origins, that the national differences can most closely be seen. The American ballad differs from its English predecessor. The Negro spiritual has lost the savage rhythm of its African forebear. French ballads in Louisiana, Spanish in the Southwest, and German in Pennsylvania, have taken on a quality of their own, not only adapting the words to American concepts, but changing the very spirit of the music. The historian of the folk song's origins finds his richest material in these comparatively modern adaptations of songs which still exist in their native form across the ocean from this continent.

The taste of the people, which has been infallible in selecting the loveliest and most dramatic of folk music for posterity, has also preserved a number of songs by known composers which have caught the flavor of the folk song. There have been included in this section, for that reason, many songs by known writers which have been continuing favorites ever since they were first composed. Such ballads as "Jeanie with the Light Brown Hair," for instance, or "Flow Gently, Sweet Afton," or "Drink to Me Only with Thine Eyes" or " 'Tis the Last Rose of Summer" were not shaped by generations of improvers, as were "Barbara Allen," "Green Grow the Rushes-Ho," and "The Blue-tail Fly." They were written down by their authors, and their form has remained as it was originally conceived. But they deserve inclusion in such a collection as this because they have the popularity of their genuine ballad prototypes. Their quality is the quality which caused the earlier ballads to be preserved, and the test of them has been the same: They have survived in the musical literature of nations where thousands of other songs are born and die within each succeeding year.

Both the old ballad and the old favorite owe some part of their popularity to their words. Even the most unmusical are frequently intrigued by the literary quality of the songs, which have so completely escaped the sentimental or cruder conceptions of their periods and have come down through the ages with all the persistence of a simpler and more dignified idea. And any collector of such songs finds himself gaining, consciously or unconsciously, not only a great deal of pleasure, but a very genuine sense of a nation's history—its catastrophes, its floods and famines and wars, its politics and personalities and the eternal record of its great loves, crimes, and freakish accidents.

Even today, when the newspaper and the radio flourish in almost every community, the ancient news-bearing quality of the ballad has not been lost. The recent war, for instance, produced many songs. The much-popularized, too-sentimental ones will die with their occasion. But some will have a longer life: the songs of the underground fighters of France and Norway, the guerrillas of Russia and China, and the marching fighting songs of the world's armies. These have the austerity and imagination-catching qualities of the older ballad. In a future peaceful century they will survive, as much of a record of the world's conflict as is the printed page. And they will probably more truly convey the doubts, fears, and hopes of the world's people.

SKYE BOAT SONG

Charles Edward Stuart, the Young Pretender, was routed by the Duke of Cumberland on Culloden Moor in 1745. Aided by a Jacobite heroine, Flora MacDonald, Bonnie Prince Charlie escaped to the island of Skye in the inner Hebrides. He was finally taken by a French vessel to Morlaix on the coast of Bretagne. The first half of the tune is said to be an old sea shanty; the other half is traditionally attributed to Miss MacLeod.

Words by Sir Harold Boulton, Bart., 1884 **Music by Annie MacLeod**

With a rocking motion
mp
Cho. "Speed bon-nie boat, like a bird on the wing, On-ward", the sail - ors
"Car - ry the lad that's born to be king, O - ver the sea to
mp

Fine **f** **mf**

cry! — 1. Loud the winds howl, loud the waves roar, Thun-der clouds rend the
Skye!" — 2. Though the waves leap, soft shall ye sleep, O - cean's a roy - al

Fine **f** **mf**

Ped. ✻ Ped. ✻ Ped. Ped.

f *dim.* *D.C.*

air; — Baf-fled our foe's stand on the shore, Fol - low they will not dare.—
bed; — Rock'd in the deep, Flo - ra will keep watch by your wear-y head.—

D.C. **f** *dim.* **mp**

✻ Ped. ✻ Ped. ✻ Ped. Ped. Ped. Ped. ✻

3. Many's the lad fought on that day,
Well the claymore could wield,
When the night came, silently lay
Dead on Culloden's field.
Chorus:

4. Burn'd are our homes, exile and death.
Scatter the loyal men;
Yet, e'er the sword cool in the sheath,
Charlie will come again.
Chorus:

CHORUS

"Speed, bonnie boat, like a bird on the wing,
Onward!" the sailors cry.
"Carry the lad that's born to be king
Over the sea to Skye!"

BENDEMEER'S STREAM

Moderato

Irish Folk Song

Words by Thomas Moore

mf

1. There's a bow - er of ros - es by Ben - de-meer's stream, And the
time of my child - hood 'twas like a sweet dream, To—

night - in - gale sings 'round it all the day long, In the bow'r and its
sit in the ros - es and hear the bird's song, That—

mu-sic I'll nev-er for-get, But oft when a-lone in the bloom of the
mf
year, I think, "Is the night-in-gale sing-ing there yet? Are the
poco rit.
ros-es still bright by the calm Ben-de-meer?"
poco rit.

Cockles and Mussels

Moderately
Irish Folk Song
mf
1. In Dub-lin's fair cit - y, where girls are so pret - ty, I
2. She was a fish - mon-ger, but sure 'twas no won-der, For
3. She died of a fe - ver, and no one could save her, And
mf
Ped. * Ped. * Ped. * Ped. *

first set my eyes on sweet Mol-ly Ma - lone, As she wheel'd her wheel-
so were her fa - ther and moth-er be - fore; And they each wheel'd their
that was the end of sweet Mol-ly Ma - lone; Her ghost wheels her
bar-row through streets broad and nar-row,
bar-row through streets broad and nar-row,
bar-row through streets broad and nar-row,
Cry-ing, Cock-les and Mus-sels! a -
live, a-live oh!
Chorus
A - live, a-live oh! A - live, a-live oh! Cry-ing,
Cock-les and Mus-sels, a - live, a-live oh!

BONNIE GEORGE CAMPBELL

This effective ballad tells the tale of one of the Campbells who rode out on a quest of glory or death. His horse returned with an empty saddle. This version is found in "The Scottish Minstrel" (R. A. Smith, 1820-24).

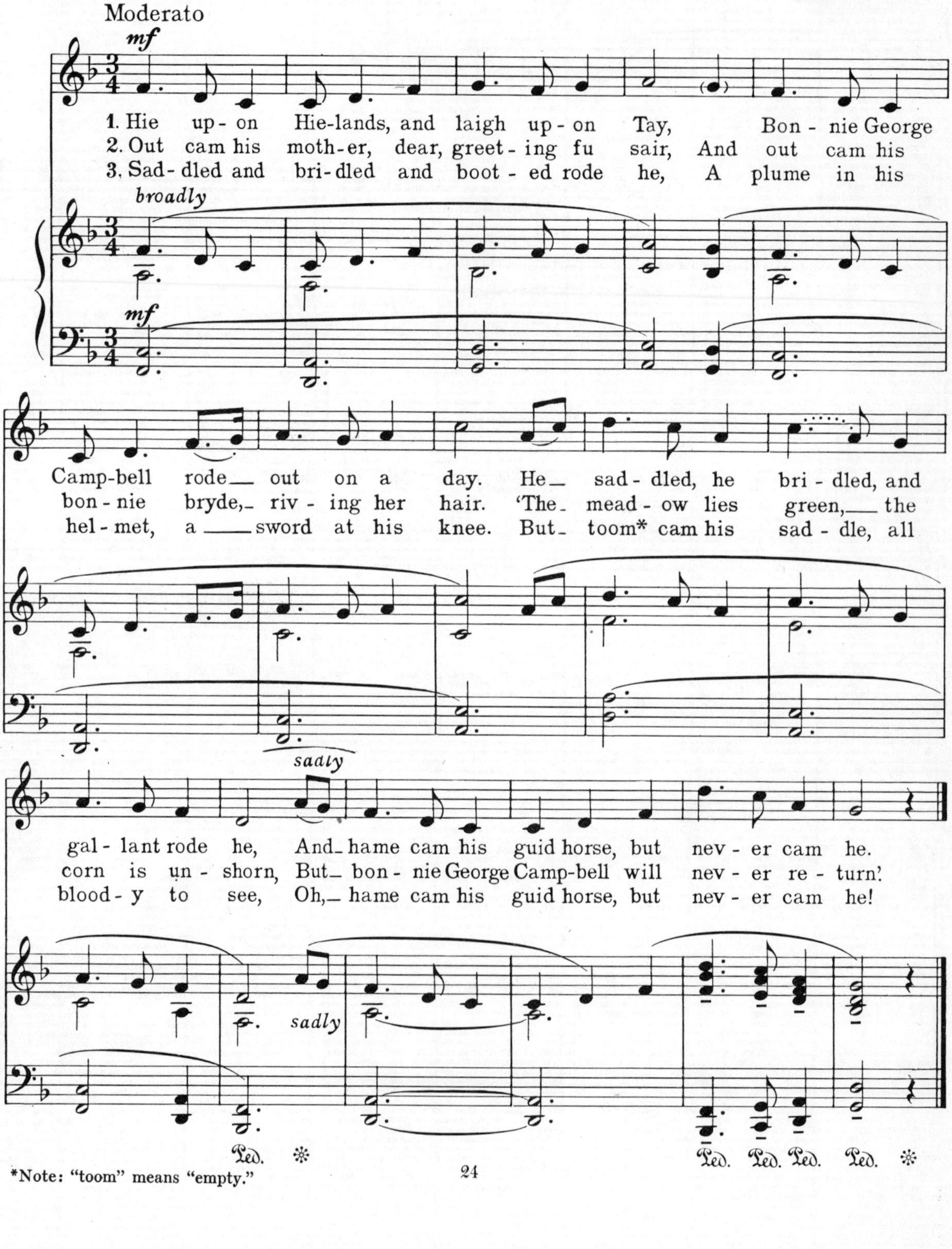

Moderato

mf *broadly*

1. Hie up - on Hie-lands, and laigh up - on Tay, Bon - nie George
2. Out cam his moth - er, dear, greet - ing fu sair, And out cam his
3. Sad - dled and bri - dled and boot - ed rode he, A plume in his

Camp-bell rode __ out on a day. He _ sad - dled, he bri - dled, and
bon - nie bryde, _ riv - ing her hair. 'The _ mead - ow lies green, __ the
hel - met, a ___ sword at his knee. But _ toom* cam his sad - dle, all

sadly

gal - lant rode he, And _ hame cam his guid horse, but nev - er cam he.
corn is un - shorn, But _ bon - nie George Camp-bell will nev - er re - turn'.
blood - y to see, Oh, _ hame cam his guid horse, but nev - er cam he!

*Note: "toom" means "empty."

THE RIDDLE
A folk song from the Kentucky mountains. An earlier version has been discovered in a fifteenth century English manuscript.
Very simply — moderato
mp
1. I gave my love a cher - ry that has no stone, I
2. How can there be a cher - ry that has no stone? How
3. A cher - ry, when it's bloom-ing, it has no stone, A
mp
with Pedal
gave my love a chick-en that has no_ bone, I gave my love a ring_ that
can there be a chick-en that has no_ bone? How can there be a ring_ that
chick-en when it's pip-ping, it has no_ bone, A ring_ when it's roll-ing, it
poco rit.
has no end, I gave my love a ba - by with no cry - en.
has no end? How can there be a ba - by with no cry - en?
has no end, A ba - by when it's sleep-ing, has no cry - en.
poco rit.

SCARBOROUGH FAIR

An old English riddle song with many variants.

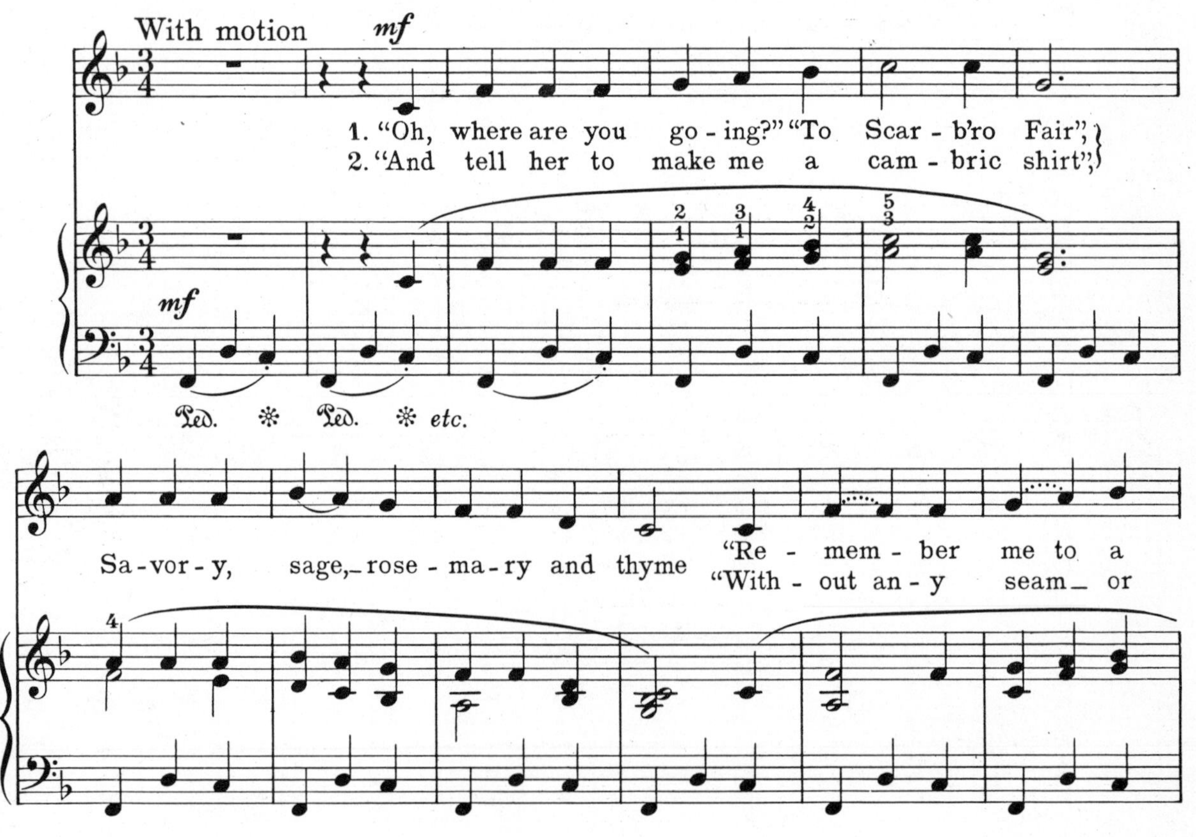

With motion
mf
1. "Oh, where are you go - ing?" "To Scar - b'ro Fair",
2. "And tell her to make me a cam - bric shirt",
mf
Ped. * Ped. * etc.
Sa-vor-y, sage,_rose-ma-ry and thyme
"Re - mem - ber me to a
"With - out an - y seam_ or

lass that lives there, For once she was— a true love of mine.
nee - dle work, And then she shall be a true love of mine.

3. "And tell her to wash it in yonder well,"
Savory sage, etc. . . .
"Where no water sprung, nor a drop of rain fell,
And then etc. . . .

4. "Tell her to dry it on yonder thorn,"
Savory sage, etc. . . .
"Which never bore blossom since Adam was born,
And then etc. . . .

5. "Oh, will you find me an acre of land,"
Savory sage, etc. . . .
"Between the sea foam and the sea sand,
Or never be a true love of mine."

BOLD BRENNAN ON THE MOOR

Brennan was a noted highwayman of the eighteenth century who lived in the Kilworth mountains, near Fermoy in Cork. His counterpart is found in America in Jesse James; in England, in Robin Hood.

Boldly
mf
1. It's of a fear-less high-way-man a sto - ry I'll tell: His
2. A brace of load-ed pis - tols he car-ried night and day, He
name was Wil - lie Bren-nan and in Ire - land he did dwell. 'Twas
nev - er robbed a poor___ man up - on the King's High-way. But
on the Lim-'rick moun-tains he com - menced his wild ca - reer, Where
what he'd tak - en from the rich, like_ Tur - pin and Black Bess, He

Chorus
man-y a wealth-y gen-tle-man be-fore him shook with fear.
al-ways did di-vide it with the wid-ow in dis-tress.
Bren-nan on the moor,
Bren-nan on the moor, Bold and yet un-daunt-ed stood young Bren-nan on the moor.
f
Ped. * Ped. * Ped. * Ped. *
Ped. * Ped. * Ped. * Ped. *

3. One night he robbed a packman, his name was Pedlar Brown,
They traveled on together, till day began to dawn.
The pedlar seeing his money gone, likewise his watch and chain,
He at once encountered Brennan and robb'd them back again.
Chorus:

4. When Brennan saw the pedlar was as good a man as he,
He took him on the highway, his companion for to be.
The pedlar threw away his pack without any more delay,
And proved a faithful comrade until his dying day.
Chorus:

CHORUS

Brennan on the moor, Brennan on the moor,
Bold and yet undaunted stood young Brennan on the moor.

VIN

SANTA LUCIA

A lovely old boat song of Naples.

Flowing

mf

1. Now 'neath the sil-ver moon O - cean is glow-ing, O'er the calm bil - lows Soft winds are blow-ing. Here balm - y breez - es blow,
2. When o'er the wa - ters Light winds are play-ing, Thy spell can soothe us, All care al - lay - ing. To thee, sweet Na - po - li,

Pure joys in - vite us, And as we gent-ly row, All things de - light us.
What charms are giv-en, Where smiles cre - a - tion, Toil blest by Hea - ven.
f Chorus—slightly faster
Hark, how the sail-or's cry Joy - ous - ly ech-oes nigh: San-ta Lu -
ci - a, San-ta Lu - ci - a! Home of fair po - e - sy,
Realm of pure har-mon-y, San-ta Lu - ci - a, San-ta Lu-ci - a!
broader
broader

The Foggy, Foggy Dew

This haunting tune, according to Burl Ives, is an old favorite of the English, Scots, Irish, New Zealanders and Australians. "Soldiers and sailors and young maids . . . have sung it on many windy nights before the fire, as they fought off the evil effects of the foggy, foggy dew." The version used here is an American one.

Ballad style

mf

When I was a bach - 'lor, I lived all a - lone, I worked at the weav-er's trade; And the on - ly, on - ly thing I did that was wrong, Was to woo a fair young maid. I woo'd her in the

Rhythmically

win-ter time And in — the sum-mer too; And the on-ly, on-ly thing that I
did that was wrong, Was to keep her from the fog - gy, fog - gy dew.

2. One night she knelt close by my side,
When I was fast asleep,
She threw her arms around my neck,
And then began to weep.
She wept, she cried, she tore her hair,—
Ah me, what could I do?
So all night long I held her in my arms,
Just to keep her from the foggy, foggy dew.

3. Again I am a bach'lor, I live with my son,
We work at the weaver's trade;
And ev'ry single time I look into his eyes
He reminds me of the fair young maid.
He reminds me of the wintertime
And of the summer too;
And the many, many times that I held her in my arms,
Just to keep her from the foggy, foggy dew.

I Am a Poor Wayfaring Stranger

After the Revolutionary War, this spiritual sprang up all through the Southern mountains. It was sung by Negroes: it was sung at camp meetings and revivals, and appears in the old shape-note hymn books of the period. This is a version sung by the early settlers of De Kalb County, Texas.

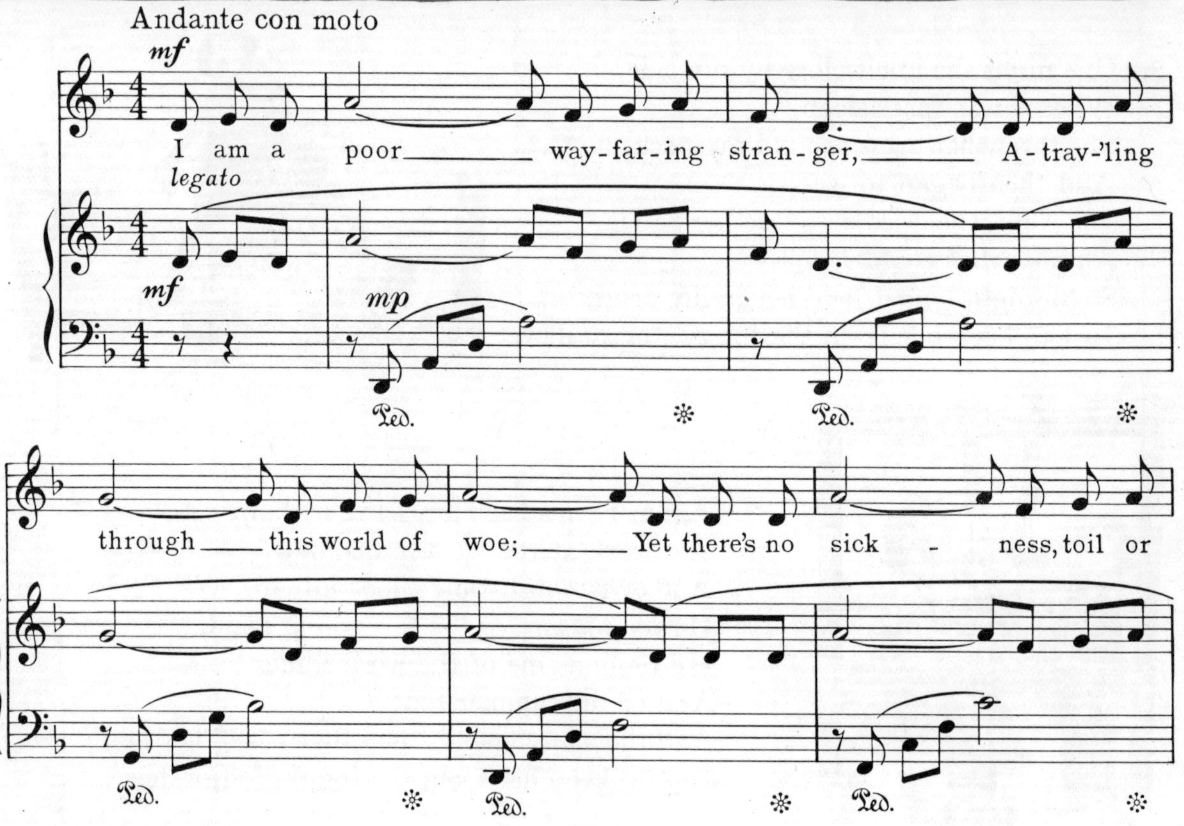
Andante con moto
mf
I am a poor way-far-ing stran-ger, A-trav-'ling
legato
mf
mp
through this world of woe; Yet there's no sick - ness, toil or

dan-ger In that bright world to which I go. I'm go-ing
Broadly
home to see my {fa - ther / moth-er / sis - ter / broth-er} I'm go-ing there no more to roam, I'm just a -
cresc.
Broadly
dim. e rit.
go - ing o - ver Jor-dan, I'm just a - go - ing o - ver home.
dim. e rit.
p
SINNERS - REPENT!

THE YOUNG VOYAGEUR
Up to the twentieth century the charming voyageur songs were frequently heard on American waterways, sung by the voyageurs as they paddled their canoes laden with cargo.
Swingingly and solidly
mf
1. From the wilds of the North comes the young voy - a - geur, With his
2. There's a song on the lips of the young voy - a - geur, And his
buoy - ant ca - noe well_ la - den with fur.
voice, sound - ing far, sets the for - est a - stir.
Glad - some and free,
lit - tle cares he, For there's joy in the heart of the young voy - a - geur.

THE ERIE CANAL

Traffic on the Erie Canal ran slowly, quietly, night and day. The canal-boat mule drivers sang in order to relieve the monotony of their duties. Carl Carmer relates that "riders on the slow canal boats got many a bruised head from failing to heed the warning cry of the 'hoggie' or mule driver, 'Low Bridge, Everybody Down.'"

Moderato
mf
1. I've got a mule, her name is Sal,
2. We bet-ter get a-long on our way, ol' gal,
Fif-teen miles on the
Er-ie Can-al
She's a good ol' work-er an' a good ol' pal,
'Cause you bet your life I'd nev-er part with Sal,

Fif-teen miles on the Er-ie Can-al.
We've haul'd some barg-es in our day, Fill'd with lum-ber, coal and hay, And we know ev-'ry inch of the way From Al-ban-y to Buf-fa-lo.
Git up there, mule, here comes a lock, We'll make Rome 'bout six o-clock, One more trip an' back we'll go Right back home to Buf-fa-lo.
poco rit.
a tempo
rit.
Chorus
Low bridge, ev-'ry-bod-y down! Low bridge, for we're

com - in' to a town! And you'll al - ways know your neigh - bor, You'll
al - ways know your pal, If you've ev - er nav - i - gat - ed on the Er - ie Can - al.
broaden
broaden

OH, SUSANNA!

One of Foster's earliest songs, sung for the first time, it is thought, by minstrels at a song contest for the best sentimental song at "Andrew's Eagle Ice Cream Saloon" in Pittsburgh, September 11, 1847. Later, "Oh, Susanna!" became a favorite with the forty-niners. It was called the "theme song" of the California gold rush.

Words and Music by Stephen Foster

Lively
mf
1. I__ come from A - la - ba - ma with my ban - jo on my
2. It__ rained all day the night I left The weath - er was so
mp
mf
knee, I'm__ going to Louis - i - a - na, My Su - san - na for to see.
dry, The_ sun so hot I froze my - self, Su - san - na don't you cry.

Chorus
Oh, Su - san-na! Oh, don't you cry for me, For I
come from A - la - ba - ma with my ban - jo on my knee.

3. I had a dream the other night,
When everything was still.
I thought I saw Susanna
A-coming down the hill.
Chorus:

4. The buckwheat cake was in her mouth,
The tear was in her eye,
Says I, "I'm coming from the South."
Susanna, don't you cry.
Chorus:

CHORUS

Oh, Susanna!
Oh, don't you cry for me,
For I come from Alabama with my banjo on my knee.

PRAIRIE QUEEN

ON TOP OF OLD SMOKY

An old Kentucky mountain song. The ballad, "The Little Mohee," is sung to the same tune.

Tenderly

p

1. On top of old Smok - y, All cov - er'd with snow, I lost my true lov - er, Come a - court - in' too slow.
2. A - court - in's a pleas - ure, A - flirt - in's a grief, A false-heart - ed lov - er, Is worse than a thief.

3. For a thief, he will rob you,
And take what you have,
But a false-hearted lover
Will send you to your grave.

4. She'll hug you and kiss you
And tell you more lies,
Than the cross-ties on the railroad,
Or the stars in the skies.

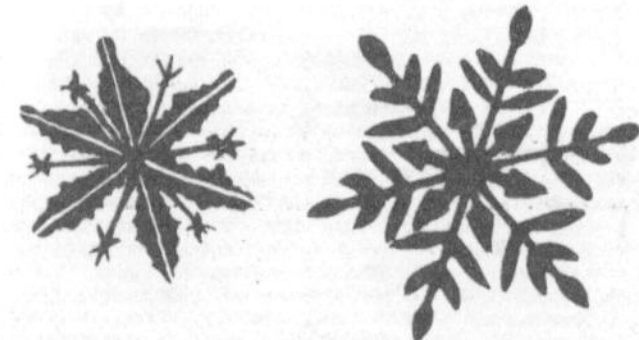

5. On top of old Smoky,
All covered with snow,
I lost my true lover,
A-courtin' too slow.

FUNICULI, FUNICULA

(A MERRY LIFE)

A song written in 1880 to commemorate the opening of the funicular railway to the top of Mt. Vesuvius.

Allegro
Music by Luigi Denza
mf Solo
1. Some think ___ the world is made for fun and frol - ic, ___
2. Ah, me! ___ 'tis strange that some should take to sigh - ing, ___
mf
accompaniment always staccato
Chorus
Solo
___ And so do I! ___ And so do I! ___ Some think ___
___ And like it well! ___ And like it well! ___ For me, ___

— it well to be all mel - an - chol - ic, To pine and sigh,
— I have not tho't it worth the try - ing, So can - not tell!
Chorus
Solo
— To pine and sigh. But I, I love to
— So can - not tell! With laugh, and dance, and
Ped.
Chorus
spend my time in sing - ing Some joy - ous song, Some joy - ous
song, the day soon pass - es, Full soon is gone, Full soon is
Solo
song; To set the air with mu - sic brave - ly ring - ing
gone; For mirth was made for joy - ous lads and las - ses

Chorus
— Is far from wrong! Is far from wrong!
— To call their own! To call their own!
Chorus
Heark-en! Heark-en! Mu-sic sounds a - far! Heark-en!
Heark-en! Mu-sic sounds a - far! Tra-la-la - la, tra-la - la - la, tra-la - la-
la, tra-la-la - la! Joy is ev-'ry-where, Tra-la - la - la, tra-la-la - la. —

CARELESS LOVE

An old and widely sung lament, known also as "Kelly's Love." This folk melody is in W. C. Handy's anthology of Blues.

Swinging Blues tempo
mf
1. Love, oh love, oh care-less love,
2. Once I wore my a - pron low,
mf
p
etc.
Ped. Ped. Ped. Ped. etc.
Love, oh love, oh care - less love, Oh it's
Once I wore my a - pron low, Oh it's

love, oh love, oh care - less love, You
once I wore my a - pron low, You'd
see what care-less love has done.
fol - low me through rain and snow.

3. Now I wear my apron high,
Now I wear my apron high,
Oh it's now I wear my apron high,
You'll see my door and pass it by.

4. I cried last night and the night before,
I cried last night and the night before,
Oh I cried last night and the night before,
Going to cry tonight and cry no more.

5. Love, oh love, oh careless love,
Love, oh love, oh careless love,
Oh it's love, oh love, oh careless love,
You see what careless love has done.

JOE HILL

Joe Hill, a great labor organizer and poet, was executed in 1915 on a murder charge which union circles have always considered a frame-up. This song, written in his memory, is one of the most moving of all the labor songs.

Freely

mf

Music by Earl Robinson

1. I dreamed I saw Joe Hill last night, A - live as you and me. Says I, "But Joe you're ten years dead", "I
2. "In Salt Lake, Joe", says I to him, Him stand-ing by my bed, "They framed you on a mur - der charge", Says

mf

Ped. Ped. Ped. Ped. *

nev - er died", says he. "I nev - er died", says he.
Joe, "But I ain't dead", Says Joe, "But I ain't dead".
Ped. Ped. Ped. Ped. Ped. Ped. Ped. Ped. *

3. "The copper bosses killed you, Joe,
They shot you, Joe," says I.
"Takes more than guns to kill a man,"
Says Joe, "I didn't die,"
Says Joe, "I didn't die."

4. And standing there as big as life
And smiling with his eyes,
Joe says, "What they forgot to kill
Went on to organize,
Went on to organize."

5. "Joe Hill ain't dead," he says to me,
"Joe Hill ain't never died.
Where working men are out on strike
Joe Hill is at their side,
Joe Hill is at their side."

6. "From San Diego up to Maine,
In every mine and mill,
Where workers strike and organize,"
Says he, "You'll find Joe Hill,"
Says he, "You'll find Joe Hill."

7. I dreamed I saw Joe Hill last night,
Alive as you or me.
Says I, "But Joe, you're ten years dead,"
"I never died," says he,
"I never died," says he.

WIDDECOMBE FAIR

English Folk Song

Rollicking

mf *Solo* — *Chorus*

1. Tom Pearce, Tom Pearce lend me your grey mare, } All a-long, down a-long,
2. And when shall I see a - gain my grey mare?

mf

Ped. ❊ Ped. ❊ Ped. ❊ Ped. ❊ *etc.*

out a-long lee. *Solo* For I want for to go___ to Wid-de-combe Fair, } *Chorus* With Bill
By___ Fri - day soon_ or Sat-ur-day noon,

Brewer, Jan Strewer, Pe-ter Gur-ney, Pe-ter Da-vy, Dan'l Whid-der, Har-ry Hawke, Old

Un - cle Tom Cob-leigh and all.
Old Un-cle Tom Cob-leigh and all.

3. So they harnessed and bridled the old gray mare
Chorus: All along . . . etc.
And off they drove to Widdecombe Fair,
Chorus: With Bill Brewer, Jan . . . etc.

4. Then Friday came and Saturday noon,
Chorus: All along . . . etc.
But Tom Pearce's old mare hath not trotted home,
Chorus: With Bill Brewer, Jan . . . etc.

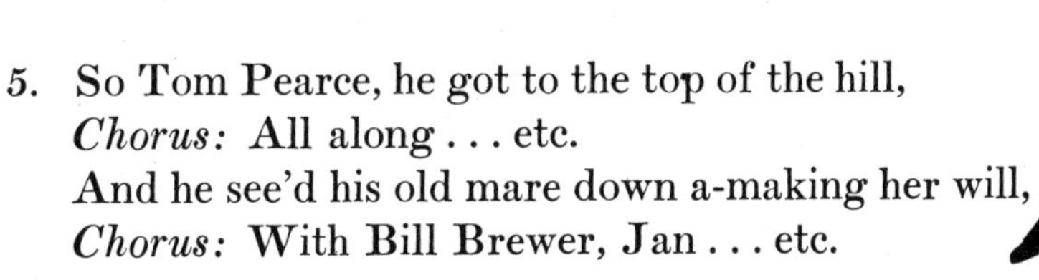

5. So Tom Pearce, he got to the top of the hill,
Chorus: All along . . . etc.
And he see'd his old mare down a-making her will,
Chorus: With Bill Brewer, Jan . . . etc.

6. So Tom Pearce's old mare, her took sick and died,
Chorus: All along . . . etc.
And Tom he sat down on a stone and he cried,
Chorus: With Bill Brewer, Jan . . . etc.

7. But this isn't the end o' this shocking affair,
Chorus: All along . . . etc.
Nor, tho' they be dead, of the horrid career,
Chorus: With Bill Brewer, Jan . . . etc.

8. When the wind whistles cold on the moor of a night
Chorus: All along . . . etc.
Tom Pearce's old mare doth appear ghastly white,
Chorus: With Bill Brewer, Jan . . . etc.

9. And all the night long he heard skirlings and groans
Chorus: All along . . . etc.
From Tom Pearce's old mare in her rattling bones,
Chorus: With Bill Brewer, Jan . . . etc.

Home Sweet Home
Payne
1823

The home that Payne wrote of was a little cottage in East Hampton, Long Island. The song was first heard in London in his play "Clari" in 1823. The air had appeared in an early collection of Bishop's as a Sicilian tune. The theme of the song and the beauty of the melody have given it world-wide fame.

Words by John Howard Payne **Music by Henry Rowley Bishop**

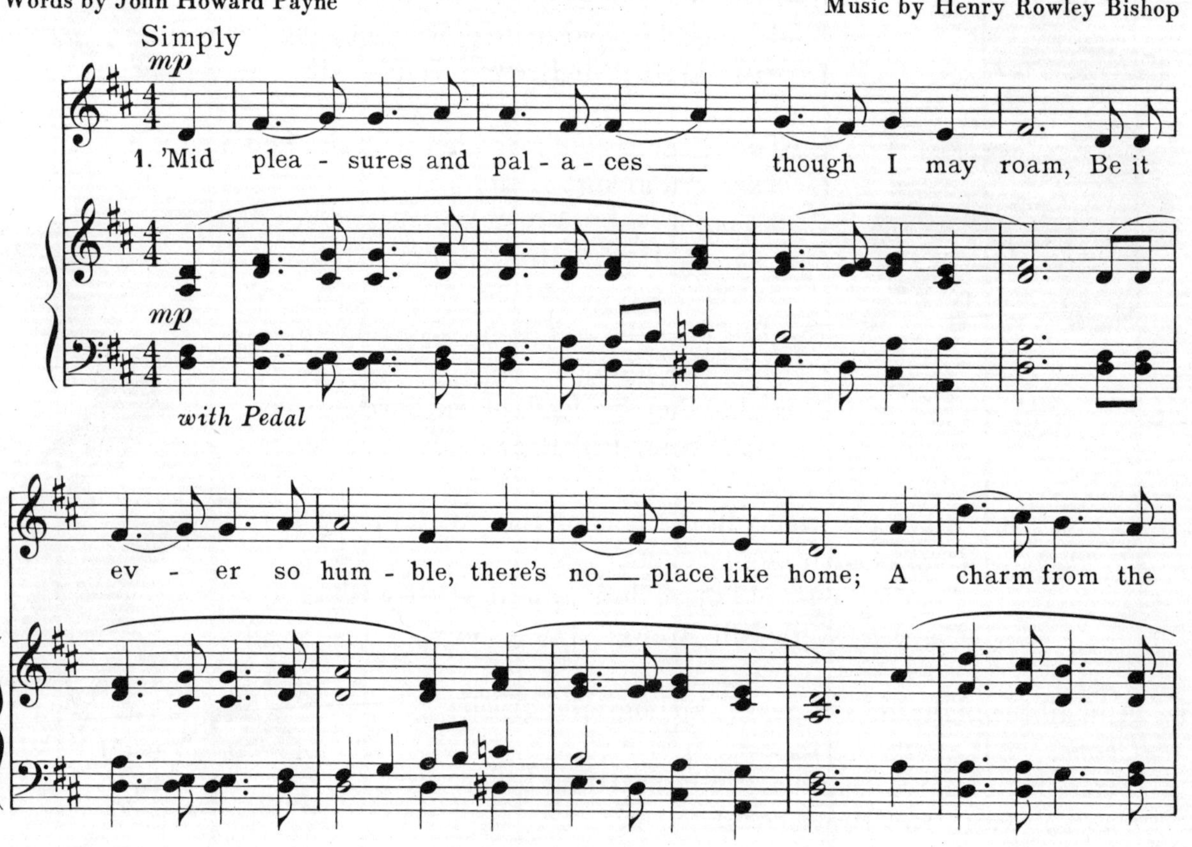
Simply
mp
1. 'Mid plea - sures and pal - a - ces though I may roam, Be it
mp
with Pedal
ev - er so hum - ble, there's no place like home; A charm from the

sky seems to hal - low us there, Which, seek_ thro' the world,- is ne'er
Chorus
met_ with else - where. Home! Home! Sweet, sweet home! There's
no_ place like home,_ There's no_ place like home.

2. An exile from home, splendor dazzles in vain,
Oh, give me my lowly thatched cottage again;
The birds singing gaily, that come at my call;
Give me them, with that peace of mind, dearer than all.

3. To thee, I'll return, overburdened with care,
The heart's dearest solace will smile on me there.
No more from that cottage again will I roam,
Be it ever so humble, there's no place like home.

CHORUS

Home! Home! Sweet, sweet home!
There's no place like home,
There's no place like home.

WILLY, THE WEEPER

A song of fairly recent date, straight from the coke-house. "Willie" appeared for a time on Broadway, as "Minnie the Moocher," but later, regaining his own name, carried on a string of fantastic adventures.

Not too fast
mp
p
1. Did you ev-er hear the sto-ry 'bout Wil-ly, the Weep-er? Made his liv-in' as a chim-ney sweep-er. He had the dope hab-it an' he had it
2. He went down to the dope house one Sat-ur-day night, An' he knew that the lights would be burn-ing bright. I guess he smoked a doz-en pills or
Ped. ✻ Ped. ✻
Ped. ✻ Ped. ✻ etc.
p
cresc.

slower

bad: Lis - ten while I tell you 'bout the dream he had:
mo'; When he woke up he was on a for - eign sho':

mf *p*

Chorus
a tempo

Teet tee dee dee dee dee,— toot too doo doo doo doo,— Yah dee dah dah, dee dee dee, dee dah dah!——

pp *no Pedal*

3. Queen o' Bulgaria wuz the first he met;
She called him her darlin' an' her lovin' pet.
She promised him a pretty Ford automobile,
With a diamond headlight an' a silver steerin'-wheel:
Chorus:

4. Willy landed in New York one evenin' late,
He asked his sugar baby for an after-date.
Willy he got funny, she began to shout:
Bim bam boo!—an' the dope gave out.
Chorus:

Peter Gray

A favorite song in the Susquehanna River Valley in the 1850's.

Moderato

mf

1. Once on a time there lived a man, his name was Pe - ter Gray._ He lived way down in that 'ere town called Penn-syl-van-i - a.
2. Now Pe - ter fell in love__ with a nice__ young__ girl._ The first three let - ters of her name were Lu - cy, An-nie, Pearl.

Chorus
Blow ye winds of morn - ing, Blow ye winds, heigh ho!
Blow ye winds of morn - ing, Blow, blow, blow!

3. Just as they were about to wed, her father did say, "No."
And quincidently she was sent beyond the O-hi-o.
Chorus:

4. When Peter heard his love was lost, he knew not what to say,
He'd half a mind to jump into the Sus-que-hann-i-a.
Chorus:

5. Now Peter went away out West to seek his fort-i-an,
But he was caught and scalp-i-ed by a bloodie Ind-i-an.
Chorus:

6. When Lucy heard of this bad news about poor Peter Gray,
She wept, and wept, and wep-i-ed her poor sweet life away.
Chorus:

CHORUS

Blow ye winds of morning,
Blow ye winds, heigh ho!
Blow ye winds of morning,
Blow, blow, blow!

ARKANSAS TRAVELER

The play The Arkansas Traveler *was a favorite attraction in Salem, Ohio, in the 1850's. It tells of a traveler's experience with an Arkansas squatter whom he finds sitting in his cabin playing away at a tune which he has heard for the first time on a trip to New Orleans. The entire play revolves around this tune and the squatter's effort to remember the ending of it.*

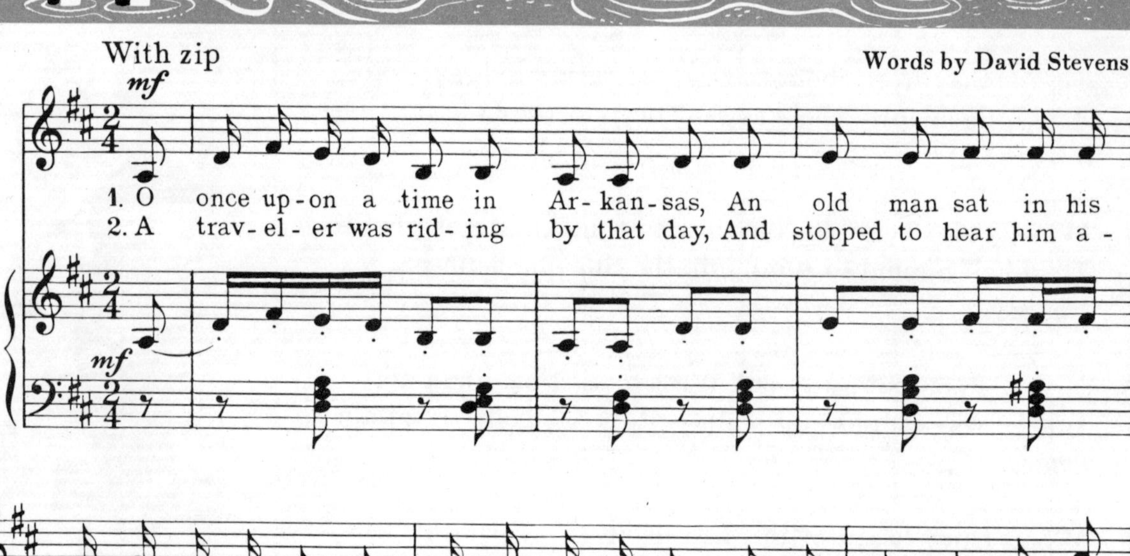
With zip
Words by David Stevens
mf
1. O once up-on a time in Ar-kan-sas, An old man sat in his
2. A trav-el-er was rid-ing by that day, And stopped to hear him a-
mf

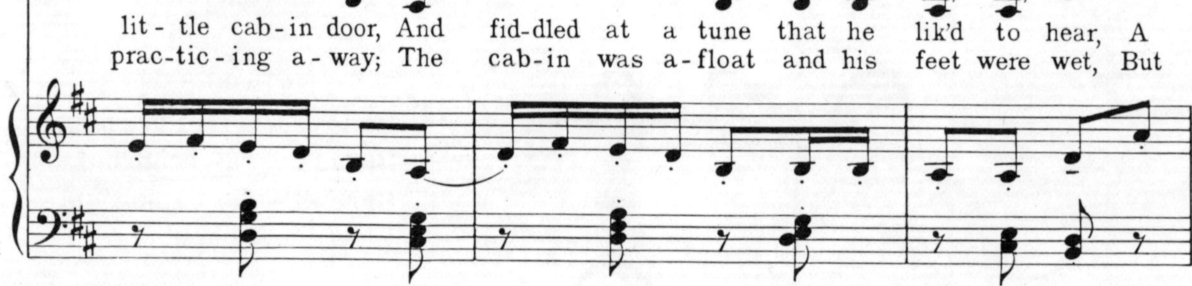
lit-tle cab-in door, And fid-dled at a tune that he lik'd to hear, A
prac-tic-ing a-way; The cab-in was a-float and his feet were wet, But

jol - ly old_tune that he play'd_by ear. It was rain - ing_hard, but the
still the old_man did - n't seem_to fret. So the strang - er_ said: "Now the
fid-dler did - n't care, He saw'd a - way at the pop - u - lar air, Tho' his
way it seems to me, You'd bet - ter mend your_ roof,"_ said he. But the
roof tree leak'd like a wa - ter-fall, That did - n't seem to bo - ther the man_at all.
old man said, as he played a - way: "I could-n't mend it now, it's a rain - y day."

3. The traveler replied: "That's all quite true,
But this, I think, is the thing for you to do;
Get busy on a day that is fair and bright,
Then patch the old roof till it's good and tight."
But the old man kept on a-playing at his reel,
And tapp'd the ground with his leathery heel:
"Get along," said he, "for you give me a pain;
My cabin never leaks when it doesn't rain."

THE BLUE BELLS OF SCOTLAND

The origin of the song is not known. It appears toward the late eighteenth, or very early nineteenth century, and was first sung by the famous London actress, Mrs. Jordan, at Drury Lane theatre.

Moderato
mf
1. Oh where, and oh where is your_ High-land lad-die gone? Oh
2. Oh where, and oh where did your_ High-land lad-die dwell? Oh
mf
2 4
Ped. * Ped. Ped. Ped. Ped. *

f
where, and oh where is your_High-land lad-die gone? He's gone to fight the
where, and oh where did your_High-land lad-die dwell? He dwelt in mer-ry
f
dolce
foe for King_George up-on the throne, And it's oh, in my heart, I
Scot-land at the sign of the Blue Bell, And it's oh, in my heart, I
dolce
wish him safe at home.
love my lad-die well.

3. Suppose, and suppose your Highland lad should die?
Suppose, and suppose your Highland lad should die?
The bagpipes shall play o'er him and I'll lay me down and cry,
But it's oh, in my heart, I wish he may not die.

SWEET BETSY FROM PIKE

A favorite California immigrant song of the fifties. Carl Sandburg writes, "It has the stuff of a realistic novel. It is droll and don't-care, bleary and leering, as slippery and lackadaisical as some of the comic characters of Shakespeare."

Flowing

mf

1. Did you ev - er hear tell of sweet Bet - sy from Pike, Who crossed the wide prai - ries with her lov - er Ike, With two yoke of cat - tle and one spot - ted hog, A__ tall shang-hai roost - er, an
2. One__ eve - ning quite ear - ly they camped on the Platte, 'Twas near by the road on a green shad - y flat; Where Bet - sy, quite tired,__ lay down to re - pose, While with won - der Ike gazed on his

Chorus
poco rit.
a tempo
old yal - ler dog? Sing too - ral - i - oo - ral - i - oo - ral - i -
Pike Coun - ty rose.
ay, Sing too - ral - i - oo - ral - i - oo - ral - i - ay.

3. They swam the wide rivers and crossed the tall peaks,
And camped on the prairie for weeks upon weeks,
Starvation and cholera and hard work and slaughter,
They reached California spite of hell and high water.
Chorus:

4. Out on the prairie one bright starry night
They broke the whiskey and Betsy got tight,
She sang and she shouted and danced o'er the plain,
And showed her bare arse to the whole wagon train.
Chorus:

5. The Injuns came down in a wild yelling horde,
And Betsy was skeered they would scalp her adored;
Behind the front wagon wheel Betsy did crawl,
And there she fought the Injuns with musket and ball.
Chorus:

6. The alkali desert was burning and bare,
And Isaac's soul shrank from the death that lurked there:
"Dear Old Pike County, I'll go back to you."
Says Betsy, "You'll go by yourself if you do."
Chorus:

CHORUS

Sing too-ral-ioo-ral-ioo-ral-i-ay.
Sing too-ral-ioo-ral-ioo-ral-i-ay.

DE CAMPTOWN RACES

This rollicking song, originally published as "Gwine to Run All Night," ranks with "Oh! Susanna" in popularity. It belongs to the period immediately following Foster's marriage in 1850.

Words and Music by Stephen Foster

mf Moderato
1. De Camp-town la - dies_ sing dis song, Doo-dah! doo-dah! De
come down dah_ wid my hat caved in, Doo-dah! doo-dah! I
Camp-town race - track_ five_ miles_ long, Oh! doo-dah - day! I
go back home wid a pock-et full of tin, Oh! doo-dah - day! I

Chorus
Gwine to run all night! Gwine to run all day! I'll—
bet my mon-ey on de bob-tail nag, Some-bod-y bet on de bay.

2. De long tail filly, an' de big black hoss,
Doo-dah! doo-dah!
Dey fly de track, an' dey both cut cross,
Oh! doo-dah-day!
De blin hoss sticken in a big mud hole,
Doo-dah! doo-dah!
He can't touch bottom wid a ten-foot pole,
Oh! doo-dah-day!
Chorus:

3. Ol' muley cow come on de track,
Doo-dah! doo-dah!
De bob-tail fling her ober his back,
Oh! doo-dah-day!
Den fly along like a railroad car,
Doo-dah! doo-dah!
A-runnin' a race wid a shootin' star,
Oh! doo-dah-day!
Chorus:

4. See dem flyin' on a ten-mile heat,
Doo-dah! doo-dah!
A-roun' de race-track, den repeat,
Oh! doo-dah-day!
I win my money on de bob-tail nag,
Doo-dah! doo-dah!
I keep my money in an old tow-bag,
Oh! doo-dah-day!
Chorus:

CHORUS

Gwine to run all night!
Gwine to run all day!
I'll bet my money on de bob-tail nag—
Somebody bet on de bay.

TURKEY IN THE STRAW

One of the earliest minstrel songs and immensely popular during the days of Andrew Jackson. The tune has been called the most American of all tunes, and an endless string of verses have been fitted to it.

Lively

1. As__ I was a - gwine_ on__ down_ the road, With a
2. Went_ out to__ milk_ and I did - n't know how, I__

Ped. *

tired__ team_ and a hea - vy__ load, I__ cracked my_ whip_ and the
milked the goat_ in - stead of the cow. A__ mon - key_ sit-tin' on a
Ped. * Ped. * Ped. * Ped. *

lead - er sprung; I — says day - day — to the wa - gon tongue.
pile of straw A - wink - in' at — his — moth-er-in - law.
Chorus
Tur - key in the straw, (whistle) tur - key in the hay,
(whistle) Roll 'em up and twist 'em up a high tuck - a - haw, And —
hit 'em up a tune — called — Tur - key in the Straw.
Ped.

3. Met Mr. Catfish comin' down stream,
Says Mr. Catfish, "What does you mean?"
Caught Mr. Catfish by the snout
And turned Mr. Catfish wrong side out.
Chorus:

4. Came to the river and I couldn't get across,
Paid five dollars for an old blind hoss
Wouldn't go ahead, nor he wouldn't stand still,
So he went up and down like an old saw mill.
Chorus:

5. As I came down the new cut road
Met Mr. Bullfrog, met Miss Toad,
And every time Miss Toad would sing
Ole Bullfrog cut a pigeon wing.
Chorus:

6. Oh, I jumped in the seat, and I gave a little yell,
The horses run away, broke the wagon all to hell;
Sugar in the gourd and honey in the horn,
I never was so happy since the hour I was born.
Chorus:

CHORUS

Turkey in the straw, turkey in the hay,
Roll 'em up and twist 'em up a high tuckahaw,
And hit 'em up a tune called Turkey in the Straw.

JOHNNY HAS GONE FOR A SOLDIER

John Allison, who with Lucy Allison has recorded this ballad, writes: "This is probably an American alteration of an Irish song dating to the 17th Century. The ballad has been traditional in the Allison family for several generations. This version comes from the lower Hudson Valley where John Allison's father heard it from a grandaunt."

Slowly, but with motion
1. There I sat on But-ter-milk Hill, Who could blame me, cry my fill; And ev-'ry tear would turn a mill:
2. Me oh my, I loved him so, Broke my heart to see him go, And on-ly time will heal my woe:
sell my flax, I'll sell my wheel, Buy, my love, a sword of steel So it in bat-tle he may wield:
Johnny has gone for a sol-dier.
3. I'll

THE WRAGGLE-TAGGLE GYPSIES, O!

Dorothy Scarborough in her Song Catcher from the Southern Mountains *says that in the earliest edition of the ballad the gypsy is called Johnny Faa, a name common among gypsies. When the gypsies were banished from Scotland in 1624 Johnny Faa disobeyed the decree and was hanged.*

Not too slowly
mf
1. There_ were three gyp - sies a - come to my door, And
2. Then_ she pulled off her___ silk fin - ish'd gown, And
mf
Ped. * Ped. *
down-stairs ran this a - la - dy, O! One__ sang__ high and an -
put on hose of___ leath - er, O! The rag-ged, rag-ged rags a -
Ped. * Ped. * Ped. * Ped. *

oth-er sang low, And the oth-er sang_ bon-ny, bon-ny Bis-cay, O!
bout_ our door, And she's gone_ with the wrag-gle, tag-gle gyp-sies, O!

3. It was late last night when my lord came home,
Inquiring for his a-lady, O!
The servants said on ev'ry hand:
She's gone with the wraggle-taggle gypsies, O!

4. O saddle to me my milk-white steed,
And go and fetch me my pony, O!
That I may ride and seek my bride,
Who is gone with the wraggle-taggle gypsies, O!

5. O he rode high, and he rode low,
He rode through wood and copses too,
Until he came to a wide open field,
And there he espied his a-lady, O!

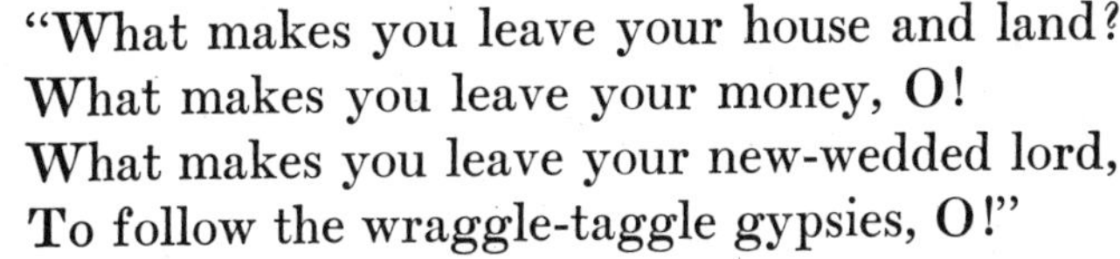

6. "What makes you leave your house and land?
What makes you leave your money, O!
What makes you leave your new-wedded lord,
To follow the wraggle-taggle gypsies, O!"

7. "What care I for my house and my land?
What care I for my money, O?
What care I for my new-wedded lord,
I'm off with the wraggle-taggle gypsies, O!"

8. "Last night you slept on a goosefeather bed,
With the sheet turned down so bravely, O!
Tonight you'll sleep in a cold open field,
Along with the wraggle-taggle gypsies, O!"

9. "What care I for a goose-feather bed,
With the sheet turned down so bravely, O!
For tonight I shall sleep in a cold open field,
Along with the wraggle-taggle gypsies, O!"

THE BLUE-TAIL FLY

This song was a popular minstrel song of the 1840's. It seems quite likely, however, that the tune is older and of Negro origin.

Freely
mp
1. When I was young I use' to wait On Mas-sa an' hand
2. One day he ride a-roun' de farm, De flies so num-'rous
mp
Ped. Ped. Ped.
him his plate, An' pass de bot-tle when he got dry, An' brush a-way de
they did swarm, One chanced to bite_ him on de thigh, De dev-il take de
Ped. Ped. Ped. Ped.

Chorus, Rhythmically
blue-tail fly.
blue-tail fly.
Jim-mie crack corn an' I don' care, Jim-mie crack corn an'
I don' care, Jim-mie crack corn an' I don' care, Ol' Mas-sa's gone a - way.

3. De pony run, he jump, he pitch,
He threw my Massa in de ditch;
He died an' de jury wondered why,—
De verdict was de blue-tail fly.
Chorus:

4. They lay him under a simmon tree,
His epitaph is there to see—
"Beneath this stone I'm forced to lie—
Victim of de blue-tail fly."
Chorus:

CHORUS

Jimmie crack corn an' I don't care,
Jimmie crack corn an' I don't care,
Jimmie crack corn an' I don't care,
Ol' Massa's gone away.

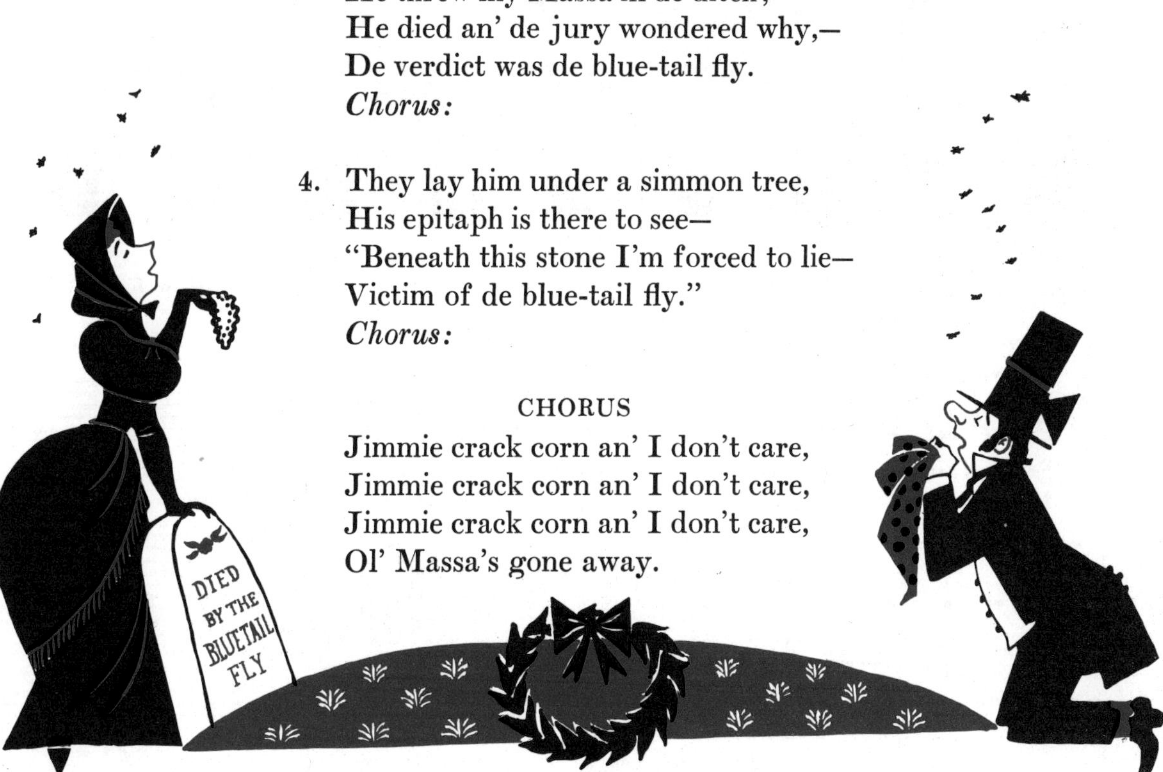
DIED BY THE BLUETAIL FLY

Au Clair de la Lune

(BY THE PALE MOONLIGHT)

"Au Clair de la Lune" was written by Jean Baptiste Lully, the foremost opera composer at the court of Louis XIV. It became one of the popular folk songs of France.

Verses 1 and 2 by Charles Fonteyn Manney **Music by J. B. Lully**

Simply
mp
Fr. "Au clair de la lu - ne, Mon a - mi Pier - rot, Prê - te-moi ta
1. "At thy door I'm knock - ing, By the pale moon-light; Lend a pen, I
mp
Ped. Ped. Ped. Ped.

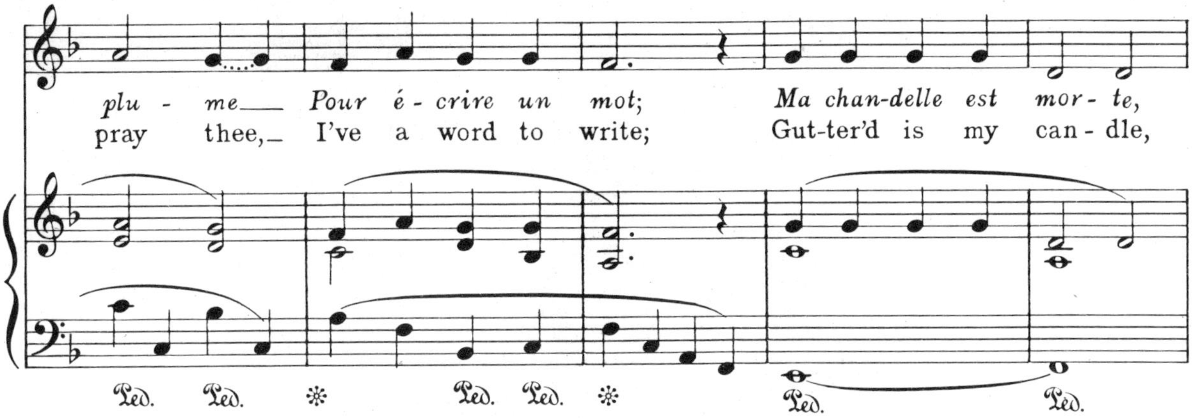

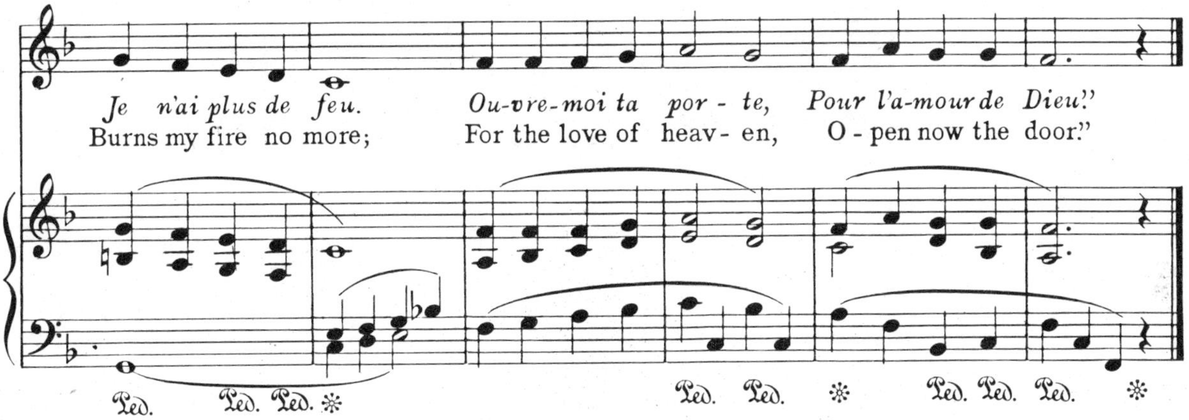

plu - me___ Pour é - crire un mot; Ma chan-delle est mor - te,
pray thee,_ I've a word to write; Gut-ter'd is my can - dle,

Je n'ai plus de feu. Ou-vre-moi ta por - te, Pour l'a-mour de Dieu!"
Burns my fire no more; For the love of heav - en, O - pen now the door!"

2

Pierrot cried in answer
By the pale moonlight,
"In my bed I'm lying,
Late and chill the night;
Yonder at my neighbor's
Someone is astir;
Fire is freshly kindled—
Get a light from her."

3

To the neighbor's house then,
By the pale moonlight,
Goes our gentle Lubin
To beg a pen to write;
"Who knocks there so softly?"
Calls a voice above;
"Open wide your door now,
'Tis the God of Love."

4

Seek they pen and candle
By the pale moonlight,
They can see so little,
Dark is now the night;
What they find in seeking
That is not revealed;
All behind her door is
Carefully concealed.

de
BAL

AULD LANG SYNE

Robert Burns forwarded a copy of the original song to the British Museum with the remark, "The following song, an old song, of the olden times, and which has never been in print, nor even in manuscript until I took it down from an old man's singing, is enough to recommend any air." (Gavin Grieg: Last Leaves of Traditional Ballads.) *The verses were set to a pentatonic air, "I fee'd a lad at Michaelmas." Verses 2 and 3 are by Burns; the others, much older, are anonymous.*

mf

1. Should auld ac-quaint-ance be for-got, And nev - er brought to
2. We twa ha'e run a - boot the braes And pu'd the gow - ans

mf

Ped. Ped. ✻ Ped. Ped. ✻ Ped.

mind? Should auld ac - quaint-ance be for-got And days of auld lang
fine, We've wan-der'd mon-y a wear - y foot, Sin' auld__ lang__

Ped. ✻ Ped. Ped. Ped. Ped. Ped. Ped. Ped. Ped. Ped.

syne? And days of auld lang syne, my dear, And days of auld lang
syne. Sin' auld — lang — syne, my dear, Sin' auld — lang —

mp

f *Broaden*

syne, Should auld ac-quaint-ance be for-got, And days of auld lang syne?
syne, We've wan-der'd mon-y a wear-y foot, Sin' auld — lang — syne.

f *Broaden*

3. We twa ha'e sported i' the burn,
From morning sun till dine,
But seas between us braid ha'e roar'd,
Sin' auld lang syne.
Sin' auld lang syne, my dear,
Sin' auld lang syne,
But seas between us braid ha'e roar'd
Sin' auld lang syne.

4. And here's a hand, my trusty frien',
And gie's a hand o' thine;
We'll tak' a cup of kindness yet,
For auld lang syne.
For auld lang syne, my dear,
For auld lang syne,
We'll tak' a cup o' kindness yet,
For auld lang syne.

La Jesucita

A Mexican dance. Jesucita is the diminutive feminine form of Jesus. Jesusa is a popular girl's name in Mexico.

Lightly
mf
Come, let us go to the dance, see how love-ly___ Where twen-ty
mf
sempre staccato
lan-terns are burn-ing so bright-ly,___ Come where the danc-ers are sway-ing so

Fine

lightly, See how they step to the rhythm of the dance.

Fine

Ped. * Ped. *

So favor me, Jesucita, And dance with only me; You

D.C. al Fine

know that I am your lover, My heart beats just for thee.

D.C. al Fine

Loch Lomond
A beautiful old Jacobite air.
The poem is attributed to Lady John Scott.
Words by Lady John Scott
Andante
mf
1. By_ yon bon-nie banks and by yon bon-nie braes, Where the
2. I_ mind where we part-ed in yon shad-y glen, On the
3. The_ wee bird-ies sing and the wild flow-ers spring, And in
sun shines bright on Loch Lo-mond, Where_ me_ and my true love were
steep, steep_ side of Ben Lo-mond, Where in deep_ pur-ple hue the_
sun-shine the wa-ters are sleep-ing, But the brok-en heart will ken no_
poco rit. a tempo
ev-er wont to be, On the bon-nie, bon-nie banks of Loch_ Lo-mond.
High-land hills we view, And the moon_ com-ing out in the_ gloam-ing.
se-cond spring a-gain, And the world_ does not know how we are greet-ing.

Resolutely
mf Chorus
Oh, you'll take the high road And I'll take the low road, And
I'll be in Scot-land be-fore you; But me and my true love will
nev-er meet a-gain, On the bon-nie, bon-nie banks of Loch Lo - mond.
mp dolce
poco rit.
a tempo
mf

CLEMENTINE

This remarkable ballad became a favorite college song during the Reconstruction period. It was popular in San Francisco toward the end of the nineteenth century and is still sung with much relish by college and community groups.

With mock seriousness
Solo
mf
1. In a cav-ern, in a can-yon, Ex-ca-vat-ing for a
2. Light she was and like a fair-y, And her shoes were num-ber
mf
Ped. * Ped. * Ped. * Ped. * Ped. *

mine, Dwelt a min-er, for-ty-nin-er, And his daugh-ter Clem-en-
nine, Her-ring box-es with-out top-ses, Sand-als were for Clem-en-

Ped. * Ped. * Ped. * Ped. *

Chorus
tine.
tine.
Oh my dar - ling, oh my dar - ling, Oh my dar - ling Clem-en -
tine! Thou art lost and gone for - ev - er, Dread-ful sor - ry, Clem-en-tine!

3. Drove she ducklings to the water,
Ev'ry morning just at nine,
Hit her foot against a splinter,
Fell into the foaming brine.
Chorus:

4. Ruby lips above the water,
Blowing bubbles soft and fine,
But alas, I was no swimmer,
So I lost my Clementine.
Chorus:

5. Then the miner, forty-niner,
Soon began to peak and pine,
Thought he oughter jine his daughter,
Now he's with his Clementine.
Chorus:

6. In my dreams she still doth haunt me,
Robed in garments soaked in brine;
Though in life I used to hug her,
Now she's dead I draw the line.
Chorus:

CHORUS

Oh my darling, oh my darling,
Oh my darling Clementine!
Thou art lost and gone forever,
Dreadful sorry, Clementine.

CARRY ME BACK TO OLD VIRGINNY

The author of this famous old song was a fine singer and banjo player. Rejected as a minstrel because of his color, he turned to writing songs which were eagerly accepted by the same managers who had denied him a place as a minstrel. His songs, immediately popular in their own day, have grown in popularity with the years and are now classed with the best folk music of America.

Words and Music by James A. Bland

mf Moderato
1.&2. Car-ry me back to old Vir-gin-ny, There's where the cot-ton and the
There. let me live till I
legato
mf
Ped. * Ped. * Ped. * Ped. *
corn and ta-ters grow; There's where the birds war-ble sweet in the spring-time,
with-er and de-cay; Long by the old Dis-mal Swamp have I wan-dered,
Ped. Ped. * Ped. * Ped. Ped. Ped. * Ped. *

There's where this old dark-y's heart am long'd to go,
There's where this old dark-y's life will pass a-way.
There's where I la-bor'd all day in the cot-ton,
Mas - sa and Mis-sus have gone long be-fore me,
There's where I worked in the fields of yel-low corn,
Soon we will meet on that bright and gold-en shore,
No place on earth do I love more sin-cere-ly,
There we'll be hap - py and free from all sor-row,
Than old Vir-gin-ny, the state where I was born.
There's where we'll meet and we'll nev - er part no more.
Ped.

OLD FOLKS AT HOME
Words and Music by Stephen Foster
Not too sentimentally
mp
1. Way down up-on the Swan-ee riv-er, Far, far a-
2. All 'round the lit-tle farm I wan-der'd, When I was
3. One lit-tle hut a-mong the bush-es, One that I
legato
mp
way, There's where my heart is turn-ing ev-er; There's where the old folks
young; Then man-y hap-py days I squan-der'd, Man-y the songs I
love, Still sad-ly to my mem-'ry rush-es, No mat-ter where I
stay All up and down the whole cre-a-tion, Sad-ly I
sung. When I was play-ing with my broth-er, Hap-py was
rove. When shall I see the bees a-hum-ming, All 'round the

roam, Still long-ing for the old plan-ta-tion, And for the old folks at
I, Oh, take me to my kind old moth-er, There let me live and—
comb? When shall I hear the ban-jo strum-ming, Down in my good old—

mf *Chorus*

home. All the world is sad and drear-y Ev-'ry-where I roam,
die.
home.

O dar-kies, how my heart grows wear-y, Far from the old folks at home.

When Foster wrote so nostalgically about the "Swanee River" it was for him only a name on the map, for he did not make his first trip to the South until 1852, after "Old Folks at Home" had been published. The song was written for the Christy minstrels and appeared first under the name of E. P. Christy.

My Gentle Harp

(A LONDONDERRY AIR)

Words by Thomas Moore

Andante — freely

mp

1. My gen-tle harp, once more_ I___ wak - en The sweet-ness
2. Then who can ask for notes_ of___ pleas - ure, My droop-ing

poco rit. *a tempo*

of thy slumb - 'ring_ strain,_____ In tears our last fare - well_ was__

harp, from chords like_ thine?_____ A - las, the lark's_____ gay_morn-ing

tak - en, And now_ in___ tears we meet_ a - gain._______ Yet e - ven

meas-ure As ill__ would_ suit the swan's_de - cline._______ Or how shall

Hubert Parry, author of the famous song "Jerusalem," speaks of this Irish melody as "the most beautiful tune in the world." It is thought to be a genuine folk song, and the first words known to have been set to it were "Would I were Erin's apple blossom o'er you," by Alfred Perceval Graves. More recently the words of "Danny Boy" have been sung to this tune.

mf
then, while peace_ was_ sing-ing Her hal-cyon song o'er land_ and_
I, who love,_ who_ bless thee, In-voke thy breath for free - dom's_
sea, ______ Though joy and hope to oth - ers_ bring-ing, She on-ly
strains, ______ When e'en the wreaths in which I__ dress thee, Are sad-ly
f
mp slower
slower
mp
brought new_ tears_ to_ thee. ______
mixed,_ half_ flowers, half_ chains? ______

Drink to Me Only with Thine Eyes

Andante, con moto

mp

1. Drink to me on - ly with thine eyes_ And I_ will pledge with mine;_
2. I sent thee late a ros - y wreath, Not so_ much hon - 'ring thee_

Or leave a kiss with - in_ the cup,_ And I'll_ not ask for wine;_ The
As giv - ing it a hope that there_ It could not with - ered be;_ But

thirst that from the soul doth rise, Doth ask a drink di - vine;
thou there-on did'st on - ly breathe, And sent'st it back to me,

But might I of Jove's nec - tar sup, I would not change for thine.
Since when it grows and smells, I swear, Not of it - self but thee.

The origin of this tune is not known, nor can it be traced back beyond about 1770. The poem, by Ben Jonson, was written in 1616.

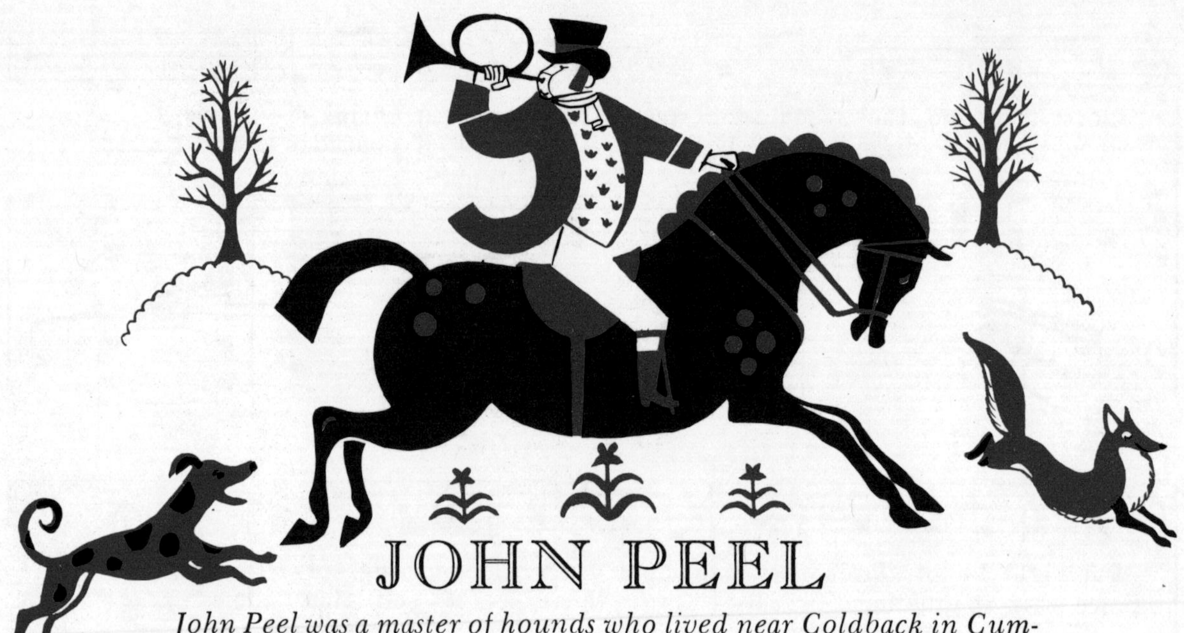

JOHN PEEL

John Peel was a master of hounds who lived near Coldback in Cumberland, England. The poem was written by his friend, John Woodcock Graves, about 1820, and set to an old folk tune, "Bonnie Annie."

Words by John W. Graves

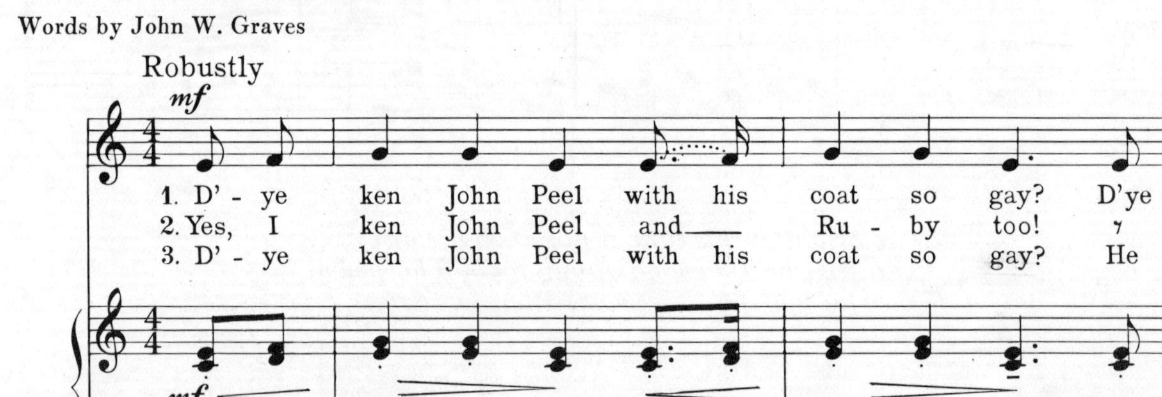
Robustly
mf
1. D'-ye ken John Peel with his coat so gay? D'ye
2. Yes, I ken John Peel and___ Ru-by too!
3. D'-ye ken John Peel with his coat so gay? He
mf
Ped. ✻ Ped. ✻

broader
a tempo
ken__ John Peel at the break-__ of__ day, D'-ye ken John-__ Peel when he's
Rant-er and Ring-wood,_ Bell-man and_ True, From a find to a check, from a
lived_ at Trout-beck__ once__ on a day, Now he has gone
broader
f
a tempo
Ped. ✻ Ped. ✻ Ped. Ped. Ped. ✻

far, far a - way, With his hounds and his horn in the morn - ing?
check to a view, From a view to a death in the morn - ing.
far, far a - way, We shall ne'er hear his voice in the morn - ing.
Chorus
'Twas the sound of his horn brought— me from my bed, And the
staccato
cry of his hounds which he oft-times led, For— Peel's "View hal-lo!" would a -
broader
a tempo
wak - en the dead, Or the fox from his lair in the morn - ing.

The Three Ravens

A very old English song which appears in Ravenscroft's "Melismata" in 1611.

With much expression

mp

Chorus

1. There were three ra - vens sat on a tree, } Down a down, hey
2. Down in ___ yon - der green ___ field, }

Solo *Chorus*

down, hey down, They were as black as black might_ be, } With a down. ___
There lies a knight slain un - der his shield, }

Solo
The one of them said to his mate. "Where shall we our break-fast take?"
His hounds they lie down at his feet. So well they do their mas-ter keep
Chorus
With a down, der-ry, der-ry, der-ry down, down.

3. His hawks they fly so eagerly,
Down, etc.
No other fowl dare him come nigh,
With a, etc.
Down there comes a fallow doe
As heavy with young as she might go,
With a, etc.

4. She lifted up his bloody head,
Down, etc.
And kissed his wounds that were so red,
With a, etc.
She got him up upon her back
And carried him to earthen lake,
With a, etc.

5. She buried him before the prime,
Down, etc.
She was dead herself ere even-song time,
With a, etc.
God send every gentleman
Such hawks, such hounds, and such leman,
With a, etc.

Lord Lovel

An American version of a ballad of English origin. The tragic love story is widely current in this country and is especially popular in the South. It was first printed here in the 1830's.

With feeling
mp
1. Lord Lov - el he stood at his cas - tle gate, A
2. "Oh where are you go - ing, Lord Lov - el?" she said, "Oh
mp
Ped. Ped. Ped. Ped.
comb-ing his milk - white steed; When a - long came La - dy
where are you go-ing?" said she. "I'm go-ing, my dear La-dy
Ped. Ped. Ped. Ped. Ped.

Nan - cy Bell, A - wish - ing her lov - er good
Nan - cy Bell, Strange coun - tries for to
speed, speed, speed, A - wish-ing her lov - er good speed.
see, see, see, Strange coun - tries for to see".
8va

3. "When will you be back, Lord Lovel?" she said;
"When will you be back?" said she.
"In a year or two or three at the most
I'll return to my Lady Nancee-cee-cee,
I'll return to my Lady Nancee."

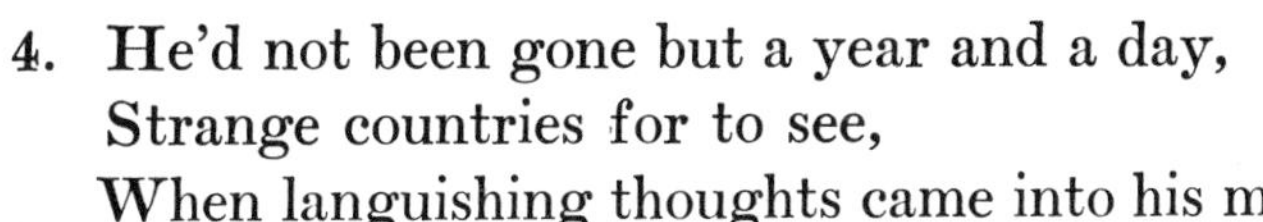

4. He'd not been gone but a year and a day,
Strange countries for to see,
When languishing thoughts came into his mind,
Lady Nancy Bell he would see, see, see,
Lady Nancy Bell he would see.

5. He rode and he rode on his milk-white steed,
Till he reached fair London Town;
And there he heard St. Varney's bell
And the people all mourning around, round, round,
And the people all mourning around.

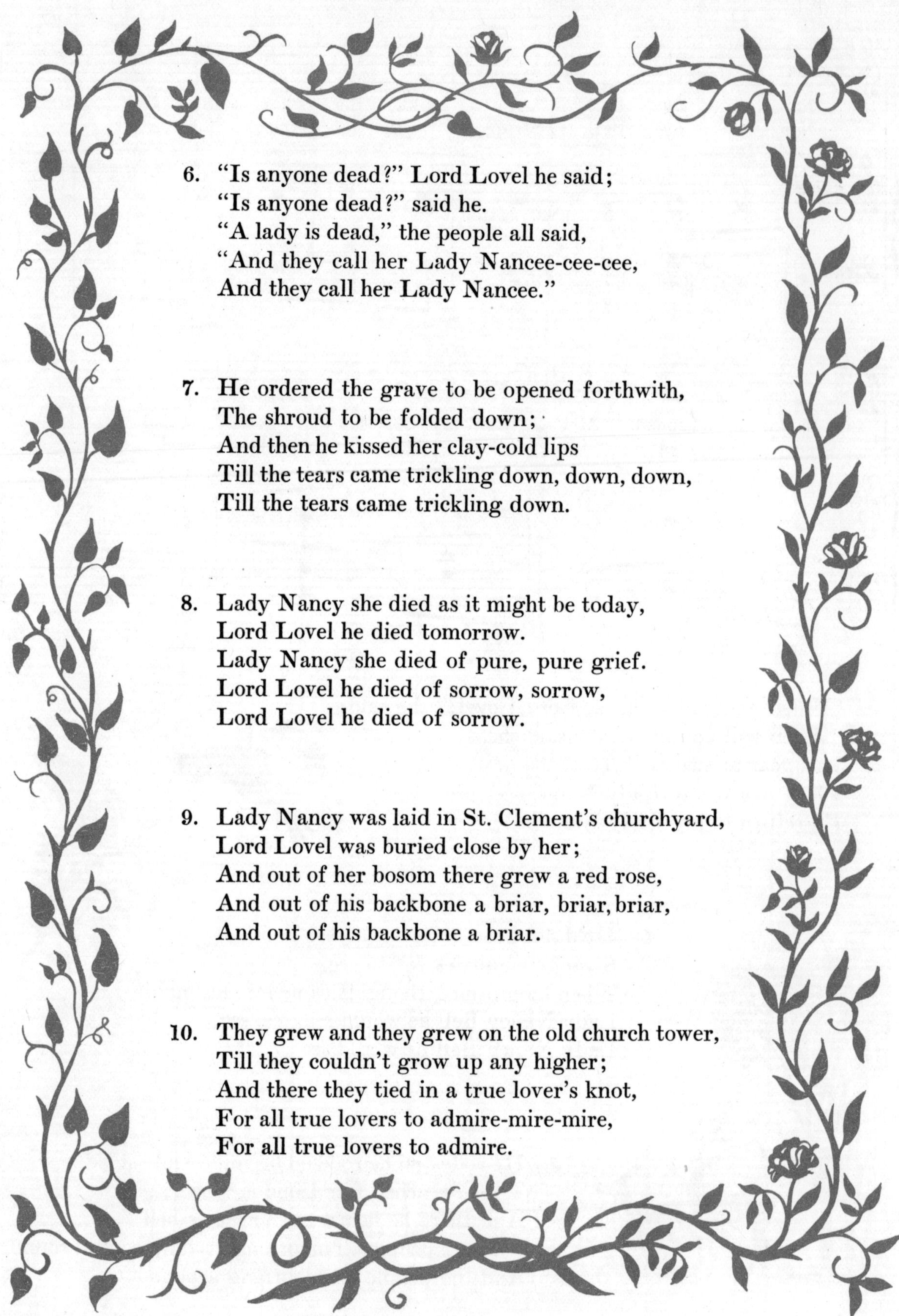

6. "Is anyone dead?" Lord Lovel he said;
"Is anyone dead?" said he.
"A lady is dead," the people all said,
"And they call her Lady Nancee-cee-cee,
And they call her Lady Nancee."

7. He ordered the grave to be opened forthwith,
The shroud to be folded down;
And then he kissed her clay-cold lips
Till the tears came trickling down, down, down,
Till the tears came trickling down.

8. Lady Nancy she died as it might be today,
Lord Lovel he died tomorrow.
Lady Nancy she died of pure, pure grief.
Lord Lovel he died of sorrow, sorrow,
Lord Lovel he died of sorrow.

9. Lady Nancy was laid in St. Clement's churchyard,
Lord Lovel was buried close by her;
And out of her bosom there grew a red rose,
And out of his backbone a briar, briar, briar,
And out of his backbone a briar.

10. They grew and they grew on the old church tower,
Till they couldn't grow up any higher;
And there they tied in a true lover's knot,
For all true lovers to admire-mire-mire,
For all true lovers to admire.

Down in the Valley

An old-fashioned lyric from the Kentucky mountains.

Andante con moto
mp
1. Down in the val - ley, the val-ley so low, Hang your head
2. Writ-ing this let - ter, con-tain-ing three lines, An-swer my
3. Ros-es love sun - shine, vi - o - lets love dew, An-gels in
mp smoothly
o - ver, hear the wind blow. Hear the wind blow, dear, hear the wind
ques - tion, will you be mine? Will you be mine, dear, will you be
heav - en, know I love you. Know I love you, dear, know I love
blow, Hang your head o - ver, hear the wind blow.
mine? An-swer my ques - tion, will you be mine?
you, An-gels in heav - en, know I love you.

Jeanie with the Light Brown Hair

"Jeanie" was advertised in 1854 as a song "embellished with a beautiful vignette." The inspiration of the song was Foster's wife, a Miss Jane McDowell, to whom he was married in 1850. The marriage proved an unhappy one.

Words and Music by Stephen Foster

mp Moderato
1. I dream of Jean-ie with the light brown hair, Borne, like a va-por,
2. I long for Jean-ie with the day - dawn smile, Rad - iant in glad-ness,
mp
with Pedal
on the sum-mer's air; I see her trip-ping where the bright streams play,
warm with win-ning guile; I hear her mel - o - dies, like joys gone_ by,

Hap-py as the dai-sies that dance on her way. Man-y were the wild notes her
Sigh-ing round my heart o'er the fond hopes that die; Sigh-ing like the night wind and
mer-ry voice would pour, Man-y were the blithe birds that war-bled them o'er; Ah!
sob-bing like the rain, Wail-ing for the lost one that comes not a-gain; Ah!
mp
I dream of Jean-ie with the light brown hair,
I long for Jean-ie and my heart bows_ low,
mp poco rit.
Float-ing, like a va-por, on the soft sum-mer air.
Nev-er more to find her where the bright wa-ters flow.
mp poco rit.

HALLELUJAH,
I'M A BUM

George Milburn, in his "Hobo's Hornbook," says that a version of this famous hobo song "was found scribbled on the wall of a Kansas City jail where an old hobo known as 'One-Finger Ellis' had spent the night, recovering from an overdose of rotgut whisky."

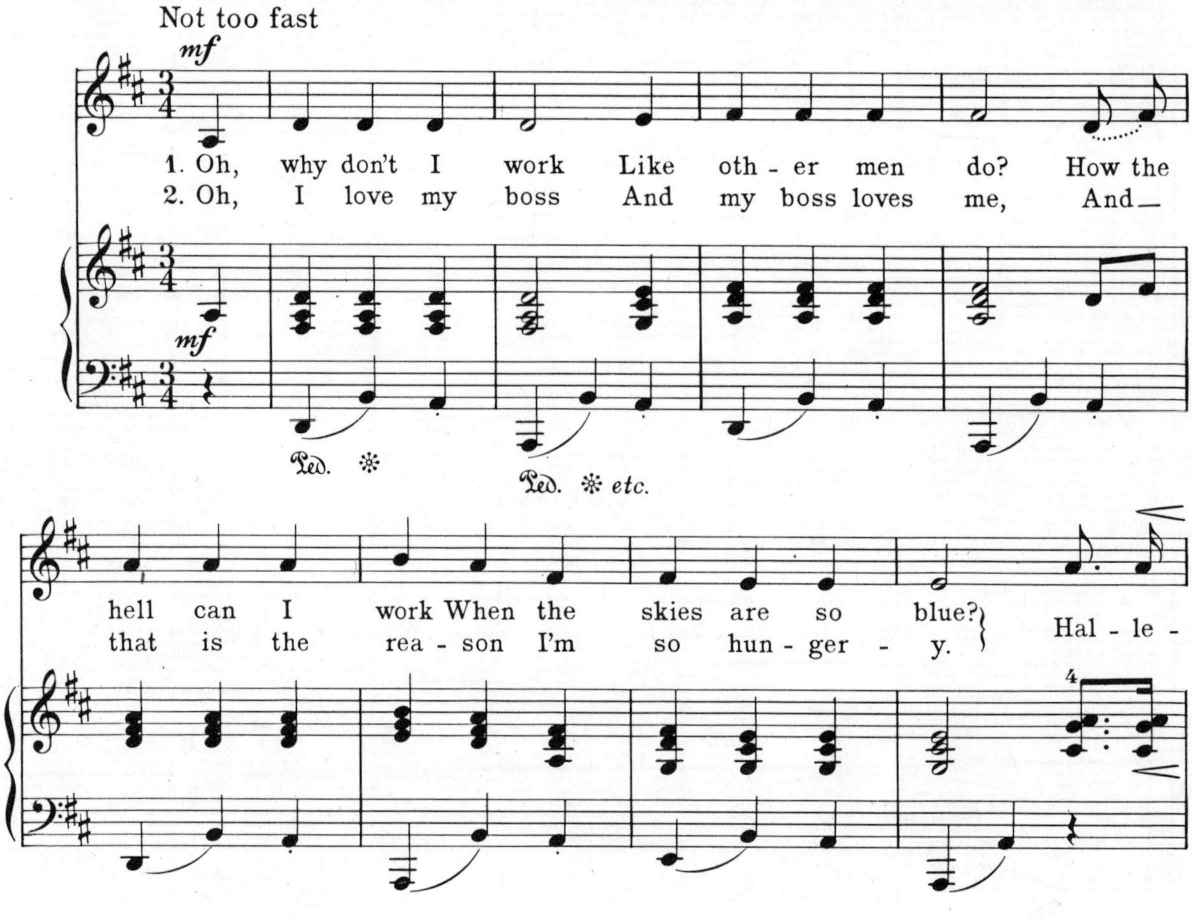

Not too fast

mf

1. Oh, why don't I work Like oth - er men do? How the hell can I work When the skies are so blue?
2. Oh, I love my boss And my boss loves me, And — that is the rea - son I'm so hun - ger - y.

Hal - le -

Ped. ✻ Ped. ✻ *etc.*

lu - jah! I'm a bum, Hal - le - lu - jah! bum a - gain, Hal - le -
3
lu - jah! give us a hand - out, And re - vive us a - gain.
3
4

3. Oh, the springtime has come
And I'm just out of jail,
Without any money,
Without any bail.
Hallelujah, etc.

4. I went to a house
And I knocked on the door;
A lady came out, says,
"You been here before."
Hallelujah, etc.

5. I went to a house,
And I asked for a piece of bread;
A lady came out, says,
"The baker is dead."
Hallelujah, etc.

6. When springtime does come,
Oh, won't we have fun,
We'll throw up our jobs
And we'll go on the bum.
Hallelujah, etc.

Hallelujah! I'm a bum,
Hallelujah! bum again,
Hallelujah! give us a handout,
And revive us again.

BARBARA ALLEN

Samuel Pepys in his Diary *under the date of January 2, 1666, speaks of the singing of "Barbara Allen." The English and the Scotch both claim the original ballad in different versions, and both versions were brought over to this country by the earliest settlers. Since then there have been countless variations; some ninety-eight are found in Virginia alone. The ballad used here is the English one. The tune is traditional.*

In narrative style
mf
1. In Scar-let town where I was born, There was a fair maid
2. All in the mer - ry month of May, When green buds they were
mf

dwel-lin', Made ev-'ry youth cry,_ "Well - a - day", Her name was Bar-b'ra Al-len.
swel-lin', Young Jen-ny Grove on his death-bed lay, For love of Bar-b'ra Al-len.

3. He sent his man unto her then,
To the town where she was dwellin'.
"You must come to my master, dear,
If your name be Barb'ra Allen."

4. So slowly, slowly she came up,
And slowly she came nigh him,
And all she said when there she came:
"Young man, I think you're dying!"

5. He turned his face unto the wall,
And death was drawing nigh him.
"Adieu, adieu, my dear friends all,
And be kind to Barb'ra Allen."

6. As she was walking o'er the fields,
She heard the death bell knellin',
And ev'ry stroke did seem to say,
"Unworthy Barb'ra Allen."

7. When he was dead and laid in grave,
Her heart was struck with sorrow.
"O mother, mother, make my bed
For I shall die tomorrow."

8. And on her deathbed as she lay,
She begged to be buried by him,
And sore repented of the day
That she did e'er deny him.

9. "Farewell," she said, "ye virgins all,
And shun the fault I fell in,
Henceforth take warning by the fall
Of cruel Barb'ra Allen."

FLOW GENTLY, SWEET AFTON

The poem was presented by Burns to Mrs. General Stewart of Stair in appreciation of her friendship. The "Mary" referred to, however, is undoubtedly another lady, Mary Campbell, whom he loved and wooed during the year 1786, the year in which the song was written.

Words by Robert Burns

Music by Alexander Hume

Gracefully

mp

1. Flow gen-tly sweet Af-ton, a-mong thy green braes; Flow
2. Thy crys-tal stream Af-ton, how love-ly it glides, And

mp

Ped. * Ped. *

gen-tly, I'll sing thee a song in thy praise; My Ma-ry's a-
winds by the cot where my Ma-ry re-sides. How wan-ton thy

Ped. * Ped. *

sleep by thy mur-mur-ing stream, Flow gen-tly sweet Af-ton, dis-
wa-ters her snow-y feet lave, As gath-ering sweet flow-'rets, she

Ped. * Ped. * Ped. * Ped. Ped. Ped.

turb not her dream. Thou_ stock-dove, whose ech - o re - sounds from the
stems thy clear wave. Flow_ gen - tly, sweet Af - ton, a - mong thy green
hill, Ye wild whis-tling black-birds in yon_ thorn - y_ dell, Thou
braes, Flow gen - tly, sweet riv - er, the theme of_ my_ lays; My
green-crest - ed_ lap - wing, thy scream - ing for - bear I charge you, dis -
Ma - ry's a - sleep by thy mur - mur - ing stream, Flow gen - tly, sweet
turb not my slum - ber - ing fair.
Af - ton, dis - turb not her dream.

La Vidalita

A popular gaucho *song in both Uruguay and Argentina. The word vidalita" is an exclamation signifying the diverse emotions of the* gaucho *as he herds the cattle over the vast* pampa. *This is an Uruguayan version of the song.*

Translation by Irma Labastille

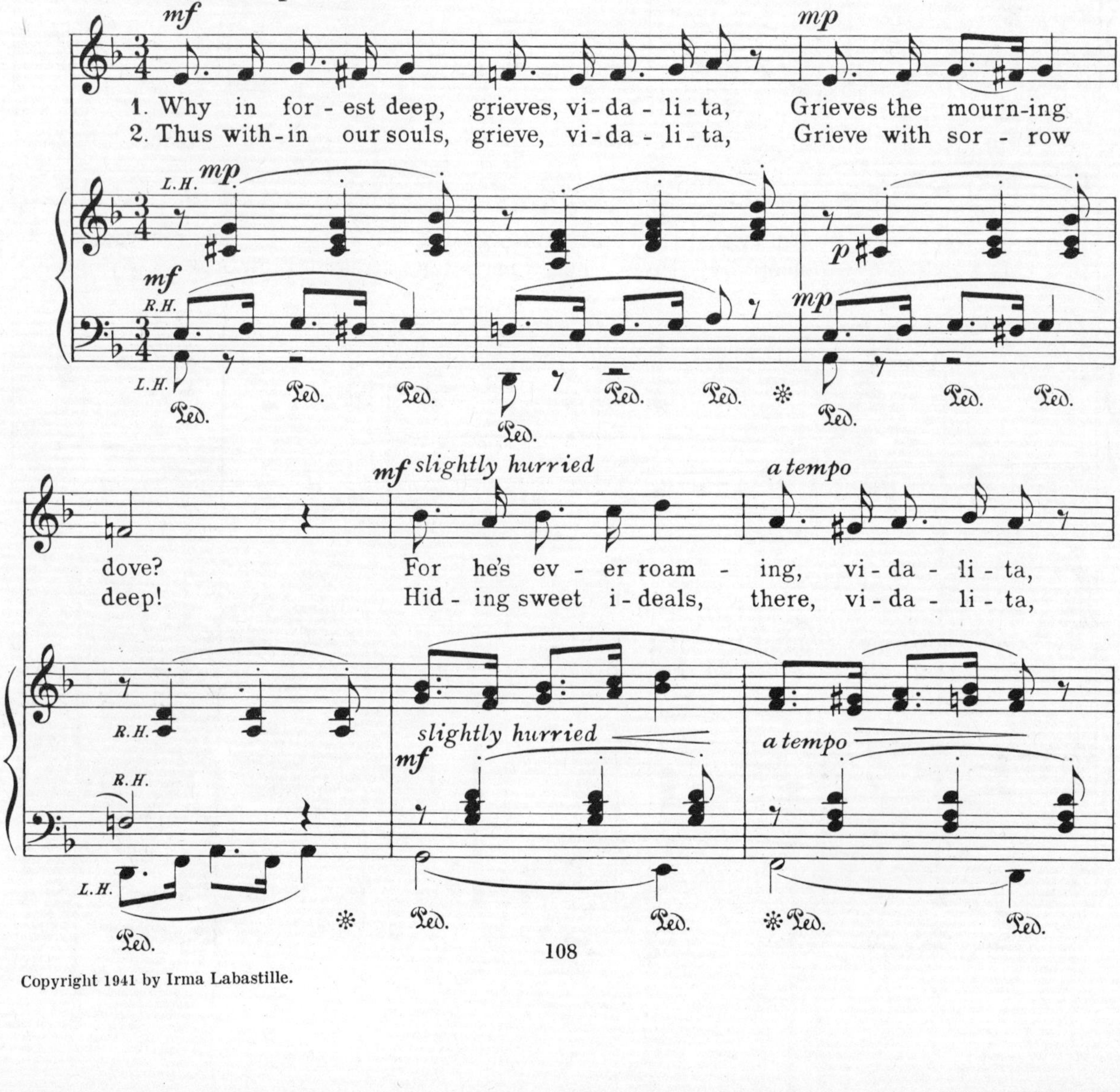

Andante espressivo

mf

1. Why in for - est deep, grieves, vi - da - li - ta, Grieves the mourn-ing dove? For he's ev - er roam - ing, vi - da - li - ta,
2. Thus with - in our souls, grieve, vi - da - li - ta, Grieve with sor - row deep! Hid - ing sweet i - deals, there, vi - da - li - ta,

mp L.H. R.H. mf p mp Ped. slightly hurried a tempo

mp slower
hurried
In the sol - i - tude. For he's ev - er roam -
Which will nev - er come true. Hid - ing sweet i - deals,
mp slower
hurried
a tempo
p rit.
ing, Vi - da - li - ta, In the sol - i - tude.
there, Vi - da - li - ta, Which will nev - er come true.
a tempo
p rit.

ANNIE LAURIE

The original poem was written by William Douglas of Fingland, 1685, who was in love with Annie Laurie, the beautiful daughter of Sir Robert Laurie, first baronet of Maxwellton. The song with the version of the poem used here was published in 1838. It was immensely popular with the British troops during the Crimean War.

Words by Wm. Douglas of Fingland

Not too slowly
mp
1. Max - wel - ton's braes are bon-nie, Where ear - ly fa's the
2. Her brow is like the snaw-drift, Her throat is like the
3. Like dew on the gow - an ly - ing, Is the fa' o' her fair - y
mp
Ped. Ped. Ped. * Ped. Ped.

dew, And it's there that An - nie Lau-rie Gave me her prom - ise
swan, Her_ face it is the fair-est That e'er the sun shone
feet, And like winds in sum - mer sigh-ing, Her voice is low and
true. Gave me her prom - ise true, Which_ ne'er for-got will
on. That e'er the sun shone on, And_ dark blue is her
sweet. Her voice is low and sweet, And she's a' the world to
f poco rit.
a tempo
dim.
mf
be, And for bon - nie An - nie Lau-rie_ I'd_ lay_ me doon and dee.
e'e, And for bon - nie An - nie Lau-rie_ I'd_ lay_ me doon and dee.
me, And for bon - nie An - nie Lau-rie_ I'd_ lay_ me doon and dee.
r.h.

Muss I Denn?
(MUST I THEN?)
German Folk Song, 1825
Con moto
mf
Muss i denn, muss i denn zum Städt-le hin-aus, Städt-le hin-aus, und
Must I then, must I then to the cit-y a-way, Cit-y a-way, and
etc.
du mein Schatz, bleibst hier! Wenn i komm, wenn i komm, wenn i wie-drum komm,
you, my love, stay here! When I come, when I come, when I come back a-gain,

wie - drum komm, Kehr i ein, mein Schatz, bei dir! Kann i gleich net all-weil
Come back a-gain. I'll re - turn to you my dear! I___ can - not al-ways
bei dir sein, han i doch mein Freud an_ dir. Wenn i komm, wenn i komm, wenn i
be with you, still you are my on - ly_ joy. When I come, when I come, when I
R.H.
L.H.
wie - drum komm, wie - drum komm, Kehr i ein, mein Schatz, bei dir!
come back a-gain, come back a-gain, I'll re - turn to you, my dear!

NUR DU

(THOU ONLY)

A German folk song of the fifteenth century.

Simply, with sincerity
English translation by Freddie Doehle Lee
mf
1. All' mein Ge-dank-en, die ich hab, die sind bei dir; du aus-er-waehl-ter,
1. My thoughts and all my mem-o-ries be-long to thee; My cho-sen love and
mf
ein'-ger Trost, bleib stet bei mir! Du, du, du sollt an mich ge-den-ken.
sol-ace thou, Oh, stay with me! Thou, thou, oh ev-er shalt thou think of me.
haett ich al-ler Wuensch Ge-walt, von dir wollt ich nicht wan-ken.
Had I full-est mag-ic pow'r, I ne'er would stray a-way from thee.

2. My chosen love and solace, thou,
Forget me not;
My life and all I have, I vow
To thee to keep,
Thine, thine, forever will I thine remain.
Thou givest me joy and courage high,
My grief and woe dost thou restrain.

3. Thou lovely and beloved one,
Thou art so fair;
Thy like in all the kingdom
To find is rare.
I yearn and ever long for thy dear grace.
Now that from thee I must part,
Oh, hold me, love, in thine embrace.

LONESOME ROAD

In her book, On the Trail of the Negro Folk Song, *Dorothy Scarborough records this ballad as sung by Charles Galloway, a Negro worker on the roads of Virginia. "It is difficult to place with respect to time or origin. It may be a genuine Negro ballad. There are certain typical Negro touches about it: 'the lonesome road' is often heard referred to in their ballads, also the phrase 'hang down yo' head an' cry.' "*

With feeling

mp

1. Look down, look down that lone - some road, Hang down yo' head an' cry; *poco rit.* *a tempo* The best of friends must part some - time, Then why not you and I?

2. True love, true love, what have I done That you should treat me so? You caused me to walk and talk with you, Like I never done be - fo'.

Green Grow the Rushes, Ho!

Allegro
I'll sing you one-ho! Green grow the rush-es-ho. What is your one-ho?
One is one and all a-lone and ev-er-more shall be so. I'll sing you two-ho!
Green grow the rush-es-ho. What are your two-ho? Two, two the lil-y-white boys,
cloth-ed all in green-ho. One is one and all a-lone and ev-er-more shall be so.

One of the few cumulative songs with religious content. It appears in an earlier version under the title of "The Twelve Prophets," and again as "The Carol of the Twelve Numbers."

I'll sing you three-ho! Green grow the rush-es-ho. What are your three-ho?
Three, three the riv-als, Two, two the lil-y-white boys, cloth-ed all in green-ho!
One is one and all a-lone and ev-er-more shall be so. I'll sing you four-ho!
Green grow the rush-es-ho. What are your four-ho? Four for the Gos-pel mak-ers,

Three, three the riv- als, Two, two the lil - y-white boys, cloth- ed all in green-ho!
One is one and all a-lone and ev-er-more shall be so. I'll sing you five-ho!
5
Green grow the rush-es-ho! What are your five-ho? Five for the sym-bols at your door and
four for the Gos-pel mak-ers, Three, three the riv- als, Two, two the lil-y-white boys,

Fine after 12
cloth-ed all in green-ho, One is one and all a-lone and ev-er-more shall be so.
Fine after 12
6 Repeat for seven, eight, nine, ten, eleven and twelve.
I'll sing you six - ho! Green grow the rush-es-ho, What are your six - ho?
I'll sing you seven-ho! Green grow the rush-es-ho, What are your seven-ho?
For verse six only (back to 5) 7
Six for the six proud walk-ers, Seven for the seven stars in the sky and
(back to 5)
Eight for the A - pril rain - ers, (to 7)
Nine for the nine bright shin - ers, (to 8)
Ten for the ten com - mand - ments, (to 9)
Eleven for the eleven went up to heav'n, (to 10)
Twelve for the twelve A - pos - tles, (to 11)
(back to 5)
six for the six proud walk-ers,
(back to 5)

Every Night When the Sun Goes In

An old song from the Southern Appalachian mountains. In mood and sentiment it is closely related to the later Blues.

True
Love

Blues tempo

p

1. Ev - 'ry night when the sun goes in,
(*Cho.*) True love, don't weep, true love, don't mourn,

p

Ev - 'ry night when the sun goes in,
True love, don't weep, true love, don't mourn,

mf

Ped.

Ev - 'ry night when the sun goes in,
True love, don't weep, nor mourn for me,
Ped.
3
I hang down my head and mourn-ful cry.
I'm go - ing a - way to Mar - ble town.
p

2. I wish to the Lord that train would come, *(3 times)*
To take me back to where I come from.
Chorus:

3. It's once my apron hung down low, *(3 times)*
He'd follow me through sleet and snow.
Chorus:

4. It's now my apron's to my chin, *(3 times)*
He'll face my door and won't come in.
Chorus:

5. I wish to the Lord my babe was born,
A-sitting upon his papa's knee,
And me, poor girl, was dead and gone,
And the green grass growing over me.
Chorus:

CHORUS

True love, don't weep, true love, don't mourn,
True love, don't weep, true love, don't mourn,
True love, don't weep nor mourn for me,
I'm going away to Marble town.

EL CUANDO

(O WHEN, O WHEN?)

A folk song found in Chile, Bolivia, and western Argentina. It opens with the formal rhythm of a minuet; then changes to a quick heel-tapping dance, which culminates in a very formal, slow bow. This form is common in the music of these countries.

Like a Minuet
mf
1. When will come the hap - py morn-ing, Sweet-est flow'rs the day a - dorn-ing,
2. Sad when fu-ture brides are dou-ble, There is like - ly to be trou-ble;
mf
Chorus
Down a gar-den path-way tread-ing, We will jour-ney to a wed-ding?
Ug - ly girl with lots of mon-ey, Pret - ty one as sweet as hon - ey.
Oh

Allegro

when will the hap-py day be? Oh say, do you think it may be That lov-ers can be to -

Ped. * Ped. * etc.

geth-er Thro' cloud-y and sun-ny weath-er? Oh when, oh when? Oh

molto ritard.

when will the day be pray? Oh when, oh when? Oh tell me the hap-py day?

molto ritard.

Ped. Ped.

3. So of greed may none accuse me,
Should the pretty one refuse me,
Gladly then I'll take the treasure;
Empty pockets bring no pleasure.

CHORUS

Oh, when will the happy day be?
Oh, say, do you think it may be
That lovers can be together
Through cloudy and sunny weather?
Oh, when? Oh, when?
Oh, tell me the happy day!
Oh, when? Oh, when?
Oh, when will the day be, pray?

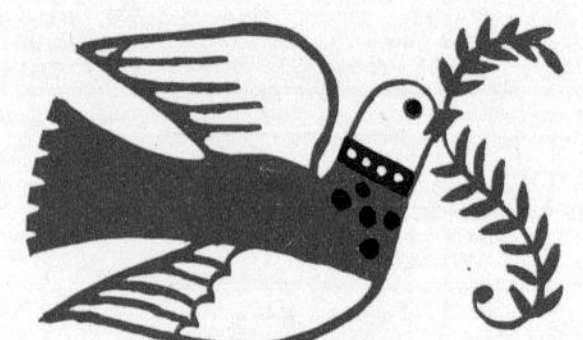

ALOUETTE

A Canadian voyageur song
The melody is an old tune from France.

Lively

mf

A - lou-et - te, gen-tille a - lou-et - te, A - lou-et - te,

mf

Ped. * Ped. * Ped. *

Fine Solo Chorus

je te plu-me-rai. 1. Je te plu-me-rai la tête, Je te plu-me-rai la tête,
2. Je te plu-me-rai le cou, Je te plu-me-rai le cou,

Fine

Ped. *

f Solo Chorus Solo Chorus D. C.

Et la tête, Et la tête, A - lou-ette, A - lou-ette, Ah!
Et le cou, Et le cou, A - lou-ette, A - lou-ette, Ah!

D. C.

Ped. * Ped. * Ped. * Ped. * Ped.

* Repeat all previous verses in reverse order.

3. Je te plumerai les ailes, et le cou, etc.
4. Je te plumerai les pattes, et les ailes, etc.
5. Je te plumerai le dos, et les pattes, etc.
6. Je te plumerai la queue, et le dos, etc.

Translation: Skylark, pretty skylark, I will pluck you. I will pluck your (1) head, (2) neck, (3) wings, (4) legs, (5) back, (6) tail.

From "Le Jeu de Robin et Marion," a medieval folk comedy opera, composed in the thirteenth century.

ROBIN M'AIME

(ROBIN LOVES ME)

Translation by J. Murray Gibbon

Music by Adam de la Hale

Gently
mp
Rob-in loves me, Rob-in mine, Rob-in
would have me wed him, He'll be mine.
Fine
mf
Rob-in bought me with his mon-ey, Scar-let kir-tle,
fine and bon-ny, Gown and gir-dle gay as an-y, fa la la la.
D. C. al Fine

WORK SONGS

CURRIER AND IVES
1 2 3 4

Work Songs

SHANTIES

COWBOY SONGS

RAILROAD SONGS

AMERICAN and English work songs are ballads too, but they serve a more definite purpose. The principle of "music while you work" was discovered long ago when men first saw that rhythm and unity of action helped to perform a task with greater swiftness and efficiency. Music more than anything else gave their actions the joint effort that was needed. The rhythms of the shanty expedited work on the sailing ships—the hauling of ropes, the turning of winches, the heaving of the anchor. The railroad man drove his spikes, laid his ties, and dragged his rails to tunes whose music and words grew out of the work itself. The principle still exists. The sailing ships are gone, and the era of laying new rail lines has come to a halt. But during the war, factory workers in many countries found their speed stepped up, their nerves quieted, and their efficiency increased if they worked to music which was rhythmically stimulating.

The sea shanty illustrates most clearly how the old songs were specially tailored for a job. Sea shanties are divided into four categories—halyard shanties, windlass or capstan shanties, short-drag shanties, and forecastle shanties. The short-drag shanty, of which "Haul Away, Joe" is one of the most typical, was designed for use where a few strong pulls would do the trick—in reefing a topsail for instance, or in furling a sail. This type of shanty is the nearest to the cry of "Yo heave ho!" which was probably the ancestor of the shanty and which with its short, repetitive lines is the simplest form of the song.

The halyard shanties were for the longer and heavier tasks on a ship—hoisting the sail, catting the anchor, etc. They always follow the same form—a solo line, a chorus line, a solo line, a chorus line—all of the same length. "Blow the Man Down" is a good example of the type

The capstan shanties were used when the men worked on some continuous, steady job such as warping ship, when the line had to be wound around the capstan. The songs were usually long and with a swing, like "Shenandoah" or "Can't You Dance the Polka?"

The fourth category is strictly not of shanties at all. The forecastle song was created for the sailor's leisure time, and was sung in the long evenings when the day's work was done and the sailors clustered together on deck, or down below when the weather was bad. The rhythm of these ballads was not so strictly dictated and they usually took the form of yarns, relating the dramatic adventures of the sea.

In the singing of the old shanties, one man was a leader, and traditionally he improvised new lines for the solo parts which he carried. A good shantyman added his own improvisations to the music as well, embellishing it with grace notes and flourishes, so that under his expert treatment shanty singing became a distinctive art. The words to songs which have survived are those most memorable improvisations which were repeated again and again by the sailors, the most popular of the shanties generally having three, four, or five different versions. Very few of these shanties that have survived are purely the offshoot of one nation or another. Most of them are a conglomeration of English ballads, American yarns, and the rhythmical melodies of American Negro dockworkers and stevedores who loaded the ships. In fact, some experts maintain that the name "shanty" comes from the shanties in which these shore workers lived. Another and more firmly established theory is that the word is an Anglo-Saxon adaptation of the French word *chanter,* to sing. Certainly these sea songs date back further than the discovery of America, so that this last theory seems more reliable.

The railroad song, which is another type of working song, grew up in America during the great era of expansion when shining roads of rails were being laid across the continent. Men of every nation and race took part in the work, but the musical record of it we owe largely to bands of Irishmen who were imported as cheap labor. The swinging, chopping rhythms of the railroad songs are less easily categorized than those of the shanties, but they were a general stimulus to work, and such remembered ballads as "John Henry" and "Drill, Ye Tarriers, Drill!" played an important part in the building of the great lines. Like the sailors, the railroad workers had their leisure time songs too, and we have inherited many of them, including such songs as "Paddy Works on the Erie," "Casey Jones," etc., all of which describe incidents or situations in railroad history.

The cowboy song is more strictly a ballad and not a working tune. Rounding up cattle is not as mechanical or as simply rhythmical a task as hauling ropes or driving stakes, and music was not as easily adaptable to the work. Most cowboys agree that their songs were not actually used in working the cattle, although the cattle calls of "Yip-Ee-Ti-Yo," "Hi-up," and "Git along" have been incorporated into the choruses of many of them. If the cowboy songs served any working purpose to the cowboy, it was probably, as one old timer remarked, to keep himself awake. The songs were heard mainly around the campfires at night in company with guitar and accordion, and a chorus of lusty voices, or were sung alone on the solitary night watches when even the most cracked-voice, tuneless cowboy singer had the courage to shout the familiar melody at the stars.

Moreover, the cowboy ballad is not a folk song in the truest sense. The tunes were almost invariably borrowed from English and Scotch ballads, Irish reels, Negro spirituals, German lieder, and the sentimental American songs of the period. But the cowboy added his own characteristic lyrics, and while his songs had plenty of the sentimental spirit of that particular part of the nineteenth century, their outdoor flavor and their simplicity saved them from oblivion. So that while not strictly a folk song, the cowboy ballad has many of the qualities of folksong—countless singers have added to and improved on the words, and succeeding generations of Americans have remembered the more popular versions to give them a kind of national fame.

The great output of cowboy songs is dwindling, but the art is not wholly dead. The work is still lonely and isolated, and cowmen still ride long stretches of plain to herd cattle. They are still producing their songs—borrowing the tunes, but setting their own words to them. And while the cowboy authors are quickly forgotten, the songs themselves are carried from state to state, and rodeo to rodeo—a still-living American balladry.

A. B

LOWLANDS

This beautiful capstan shanty is based on an early Scottish ballad.

Slowly, with great feeling
mp Solo
1. I dreamed a dream the oth - er night,
(2) me at my bed - side,
mp
Ped.

Chorus
Solo
Low - lands, Low-lands, a - way my John, My love she came all dressed in white,
All dressed in white like some fair bride,
with great intensity
f
p
Ped. Ped. *
Chorus
My— Low - lands a - way. 2. She came to
Broadly
f
mp
Ped. * Ped. *

3. And bravely in her bosom fair,
Chorus: Lowlands, Lowlands, away my John,
A red, red rose my love did wear,
Chorus: My Lowlands away.

4. She made no sound, no word she said,
Chorus: Lowlands, Lowlands, away my John,
And then I knew my love was dead,
Chorus: My Lowlands away.

Lustily
1. Yeo, heave ho! 'Round the cap - stan go;
2. Yeo, heave ho! Cheer - i - ly we go,
Ped. * Ped. *

YEO, HEAVE HO!

A capstan shanty used in hoisting anchor. Colcord says, "The cable was wound round the barrel of the capstan and the men walked steadily round and round it, pushing the capstan bars before them."

Heave, men with a will, Tramp, and tramp it still! The
The

anchor must be weighed, The anchor must be weighed. Yeo
anchor grips the ground, The anchor grips the ground.

Chorus

ho! heave ho! Yeo ho! heave ho!

3. Yeo, heave ho! raise her from below,
Heave, men, with a will,
Tramp, and tramp it still;
The anchor's off the ground
And we are outward bound.

4. Yeo, heave ho! round the capstan go,
Heave, men, with a will,
Tramp, and tramp it still;
The anchor now is weighed,
The anchor now is weighed.

CHORUS

Yeo ho, heave ho!
Yeo ho, heave ho!

SHENANDOAH

A capstan shanty. "Shenandoah" was originally a ballad. It told the story of a white trader who courted the daughter of an Indian chieftain, Shenandoah, and bore her away in his canoe across the wide Missouri. This is Captain's Whall's version. He says, "The song probably came from the American or Canadian voyageurs, who were great singers."

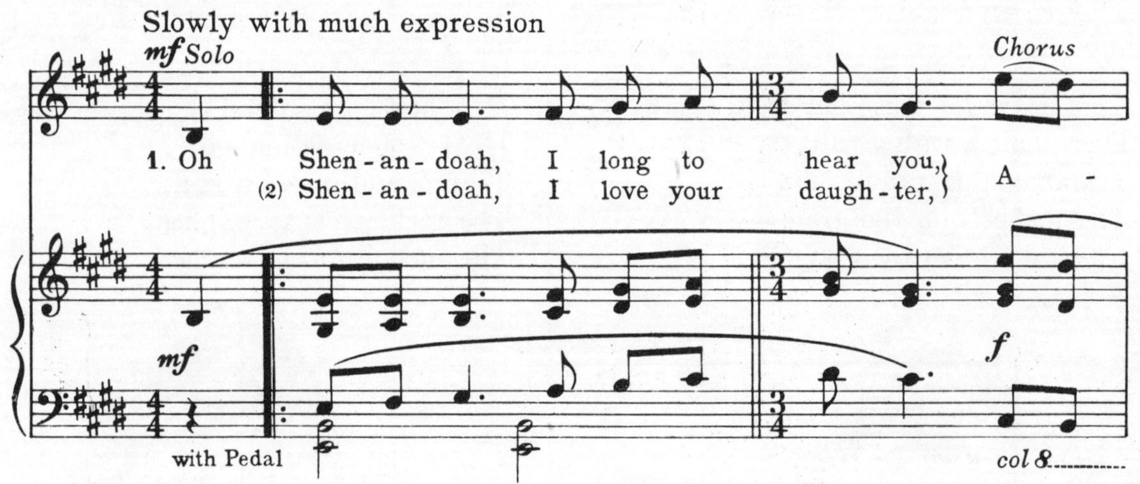
Slowly with much expression
mf Solo
Chorus
1. Oh Shen - an - doah, I long to hear you,
(2) Shen - an - doah, I love your daugh - ter,
A -
mf
f
with Pedal
col 8

Solo

way you roll-ing riv-er. Oh Shen-an-doah, I long to
Oh Shen-an-doah, I love your

mf

8

Chorus

hear you, } A - way I'm bound to go, 'Cross the wide Mis-sou-ri. 2. Oh
daugh-ter, }

f *dim.*

col 8

3. Oh Shenandoah, I'm bound to leave you,
Chorus: Away, you rolling river.
Oh Shenandoah, I'll not deceive you,
Chorus: Away I'm bound to go,
'Cross the wide Missouri.

4. Oh Shenandoah, I long to hear you,
Chorus: Away, you rolling river.
Oh Shenandoah, I long to hear you,
Chorus: Away I'm bound to go,
'Cross the wide Missouri.

DRILL, YE TARRIERS, DRILL!

In the eighties, much of the unskilled labor on our railroads was done by Irishmen, called tarriers. These tarriers, corresponding to the English navvies, were stationed beside the steam drills to remove loosened rock. Thomas Casey, himself a tarrier in a blasting gang, tells of the hardships of the rock-drilling vocation.

Words and Music by Thomas Casey

Ponderously — *with heavy accent*

1. Ev-'ry morn-ing at sev-en o-clock There were twen-ty tar-ri-ers a-work-ing at the rock, And the boss comes a-long, and he says, kape still, And come down heav-y on the
2. The boss was a fine man down to the ground, And he mar-ried a la-dy six feet round. She baked good bread and she baked it well, But she baked it hard as the

Chorus
cast - i-ron drill, And drill, ye tar-ri-ers, drill!
holes in — hell, And drill, ye tar-ri-ers, drill!
Drill, ye tar-ri-ers, drill! It's
work all day for sugar in your tay; Down be-hind of the rail-way, And
drill, ye tar-ri-ers, drill, and blast! and fire!
mf
f

3. The new foreman was Jean McCann,
By God, he was a blame mean man.
Last week a premature blast went off,
And a mile in the air went big Jim Goff,
And drill, ye tarriers, drill!
Chorus:

4. When the next pay day came round,
Jim Goff a dollar short was found.
When he asked, "What for?" came this reply,
"You're docked for the time you was up in the sky."
And drill, ye tarriers, drill!
Chorus:

CHORUS

Drill, ye tarriers, drill!
It's work all day
For sugar in your tay;
Down behind of the railway,
And drill, ye tarriers, drill,
And blast! and fire!

THE RIO GRANDE

A capstan shanty. This "outward bound" shanty dates back to the period of the Mexican War when many Yankee ships were delivering contraband below the Rio Grande.

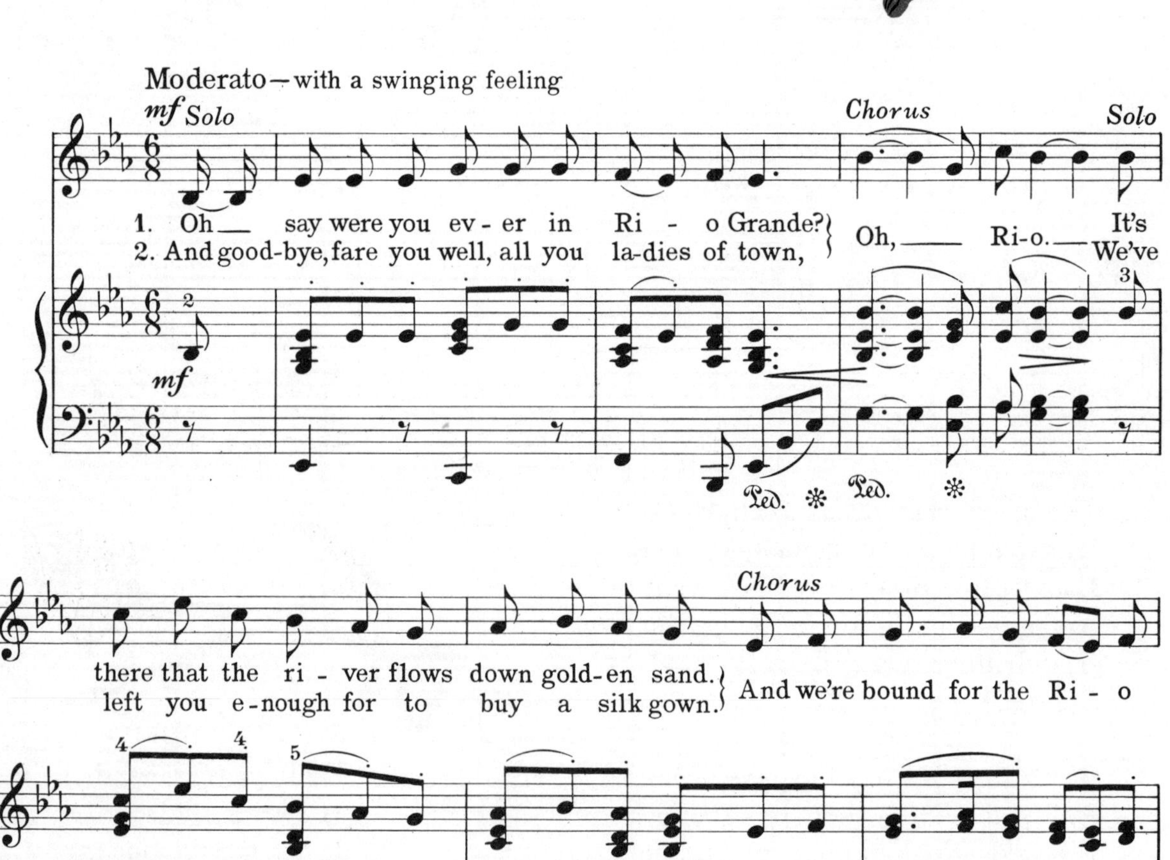
Moderato—with a swinging feeling
mf Solo
Chorus
Solo
1. Oh— say were you ev - er in Ri - o Grande?
2. And good-bye, fare you well, all you la-dies of town,
Oh,— Ri-o.— It's
We've
there that the ri - ver flows down gold-en sand.
left you e-nough for to buy a silk gown.
Chorus
And we're bound for the Ri - o

Grande. Then a - way, love,_ a - way. Way_ down Ri-o,_ So
p dolce
p
f
fare_ ye well_ my pret-ty young gel, For we're bound for the Ri - o Grande.

3. So it's pack up your donkey and get under way,
Chorus: Oh, Rio.
The girls we are leaving can take our half-pay.
Chorus: And we're bound . . . etc. . . .

4. Now you Bowery ladies, we'd have you to know,
Chorus: Oh, Rio.
We're bound to the Southward, O Lord, let us go.

CHORUS

And we're bound for the Rio Grande.
Then away, love, away.
Way down Rio,
So fare ye well, my pretty gel,
For we're bound for the Rio Grande.

CASEY JONES

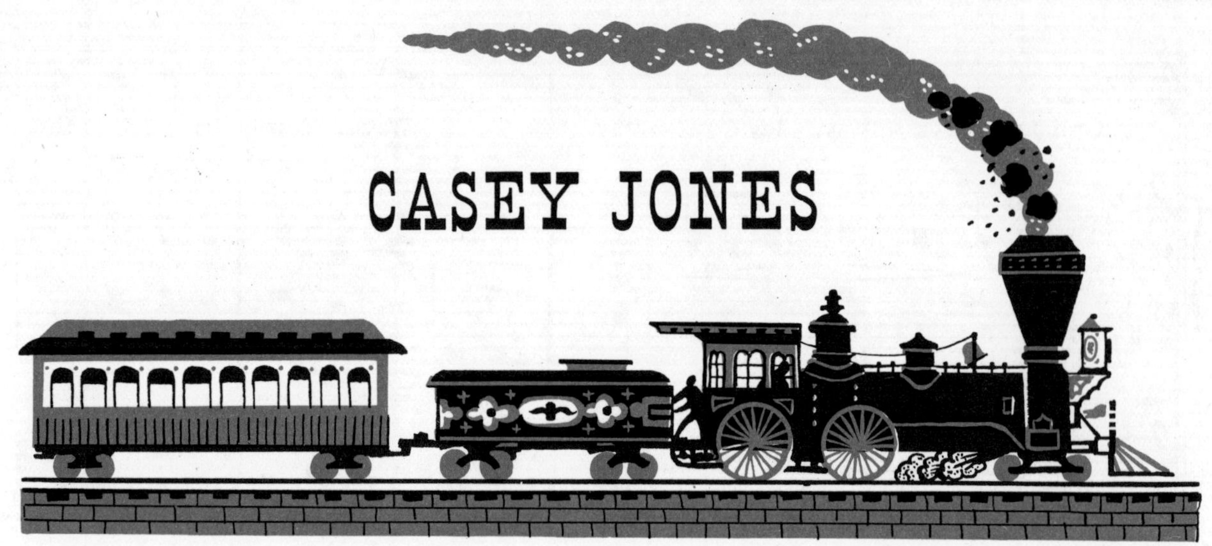

This is the most famous of all railroad songs. At the time of the tragedy, according to one legend, Casey, throttle-puller of the Illinois Central's crack "Cannonball," was driving No. 382, making a run for a friend who was ill. The train was wrecked at Vaughan, Mississippi, and Casey died at the throttle.

Words by T. Lawrence Seibert

Music by Eddie Newton

Rather fast
mf
1. Come all you round-ers that want to hear The
cal-ler called Cas-ey at half-past four, He
mf
sto-ry of a brave en-gi-neer. Cas-ey Jones was the
kissed his wife at the sta-tion door, He mount-ed to the cab-in with the

round - er's name, On a big eight wheel-er, boys, he won his fame. The
or-ders in his hand, And he took his fare-well trip to that prom-is'd land.
Ped.
Ped.
Chorus
Cas-ey Jones mount-ed to his cab-in, Cas-ey Jones with his
staccato
or-ders in his hand. Cas-ey Jones mount-ed to his cab-in, And he
took his fare - well trip to that prom - is'd land.

2. When he pulled up that Reno hill,
He whistled for the crossing with an awful shrill;
The switchman knew by the engine's moan
That the man at the throttle was Casey Jones.
He looked at his water and his water was low;
He looked at his watch and his watch was slow;
He turned to his fireman and this is what he said,
Boy, we're going to reach Frisco, but we'll all be dead.

CHORUS

Casey Jones—going to reach Frisco,
Casey Jones—but we'll all be dead,
Casey Jones—going to reach Frisco,
We're going to reach Frisco, but we'll all be dead.

3. So turn on your water and shovel in your coal,
Stick your head out the window, watch those drivers roll;
I'll drive her till she leaves the rail,
For I'm eight hours late by that Western Mail.
When he was within six miles of the place,
There number four stared him straight in the face.
He turned to his fireman, said, "Jim, you'd better jump,
For there're two locomotives that are going to bump."

CHORUS

Casey Jones—two locomotives,
Casey Jones—going to bump,
Casey Jones—two locomotives,
There're two locomotives that are going to bump.

4. Casey said just before he died,
There're two more roads I would like to ride."
The fireman said, "Which ones can they be?"
"Oh, the Northern Pacific and the Santa Fe."
Mrs. Jones sat at her bed a-sighing
Just to hear the news that her Casey was dying.
"Hush up children, and quit your cryin',
For you've got another poppa on the Salt Lake Line."

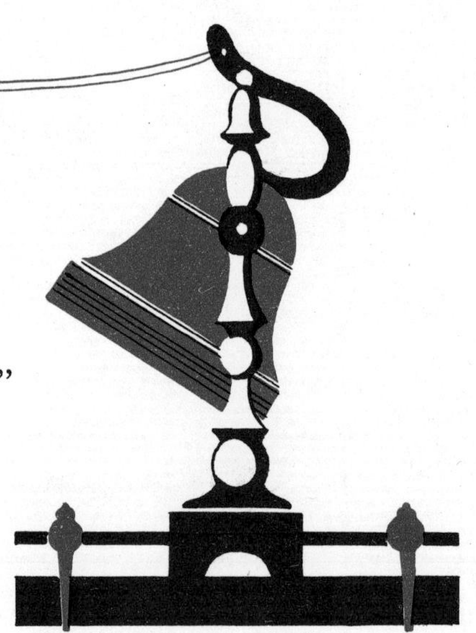

CHORUS

Casey Jones—got another poppa.
Casey Jones—on the Salt Lake Line,
Casey Jones—got another poppa,
For you've got another poppa on the Salt Lake Line.

HAUL AWAY, JOE

A short-drag shanty, "consecrated by usage to the sheeting home of the foresail." On the word "Joe," all hands gave a mighty pull.

Moderato – with weighty accents

f Solo
1. Way, haul a - way, we'll haul a - way the bow - lin'
2. Once I had a col - ored girl, and she was fat and laz - y.

f
5 2 1 2

Chorus
Way, haul a - way, we'll haul a - way, Joe.

3. Then I had a Spanish girl, she nearly druv me crazy.
4. But now I've got a Yankee girl, and she is just a daisy.
5. King Louis was the King of France afore the revolution.
6. But Louis got his head cut off, which spoiled his constitution.
7. Oh, when I was a little boy, and so my mother told me,
8. That if I didn't kiss the girls my lips would all go mouldy.
9. Way haul away, we'll hang and haul together.

CHORUS: Way, haul away, we'll haul away, Joe.

RED RIVER VALLEY

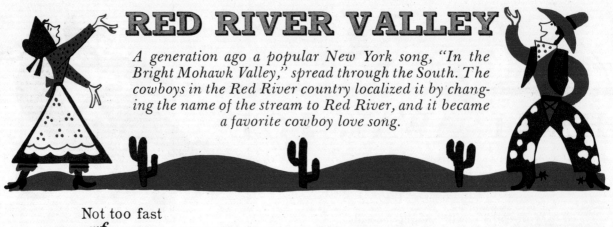

A generation ago a popular New York song, "In the Bright Mohawk Valley," spread through the South. The cowboys in the Red River country localized it by changing the name of the stream to Red River, and it became a favorite cowboy love song.

Not too fast

mf

1. From this val - ley they say you are go - ing,____ We will
2. Won't you think of the val - ley you're leav - ing?____ Oh, how

mf

with Pedal

miss your bright eyes and sweet smile, For they say you are tak - ing the
lone - ly, how sad it will be, Oh__ think of the fond heart you're

sun - shine,____ That__ bright - ens our path - way a - while.____
break - ing,____ And the grief you are caus - ing__ me.____

Chorus

Come and sit by my side if you love me, — Do not
has - ten to bid me a - dieu, But re - mem - ber the Red Riv - er
Val - ley, — *p* And the girl that has loved you so true. —

3.

From this valley they say you are going,
When you go, may your darling go, too?
Would you leave her behind unprotected
When she loves no other but you?
Chorus:

4.

I have promised you, darling, that never
Will a word from my lips cause you pain;
And my life, it will be yours forever
If you only will love me again.
Chorus:

CHORUS

Come and sit by my side if you love me,
Do not hasten to bid me adieu,
But remember the Red River Valley,
And the girl that has loved you so true.

I Been Wukkin' on de Railroad

The origin of this song, picturing the life of the Negro railroad hand in the South, is not known. It may be a genuine folk song, or it may have originated in some tramp minstrel show.

Moderato
mf
1. Oh, I was bo'n in Mo-bile town, I'm wuk-kin' on de lev-ee. All day I roll de cot-ton down, A-wuk-kin' on de lev-ee.
2. I use' to have a dog name' Bill, A-wuk-kin' on de lev-ee. He run a-way, but I'm here still, A-wuk-kin' on de lev-ee.
With rhythm
mf Chorus
I been wuk-kin' on de rail-road all de live-long day,
non legato

I been wuk - kin' on de rail - road to pass de time a - way.

Doan' yo' hyar de whis - tle blow - in'? Rise up so ear - ly in de mawn.

Doan' yo' hyar de Cap - 'n shout - in', "Di - nah, blow yo' hawn."

3. Dat li'l ole dog up an' beg,
A-wukkin' on de levee,
Till I done give him chicken leg,
A-wukkin' on de levee.
Chorus:

4. I once did know a girl named Grace,
While wukkin' on de levee,
She done bring me to dis sad disgrace,
A-wukkin' on de levee.
Chorus:

PADDY WORKS ON THE ERIE

Gangs of pick and shovel men came from Ireland in the 1850's to work on the building of our railroads. This is a jovial but heartfelt protest at the monotony and hardships of the life they led.

Moderato — with a lilt
mf
1. In eight - een hun-dred and for - ty one___ I put me cord - 'roy
2. When we left Ire - land to come here, To spend_ our lat - ter
mf
breech-es on, I put me cord-'roy breech-es on To work up - on the
days in cheer, Our boss-es they did drink strong beer, While Pat worked on the

Chorus
mp
rail - way.
rail - way.
Fil-le-me-oo - re - i - re-ay, Fil-le-me-oo - re -
mp
i - re-ay, Fil-le-me-oo-re - i - re-ay, To work up-on the rail-way.
cresc.
f
cresc.
f

3. The contractor's name it was Tom King,
He kept a store to rob the men,
A Yankee clerk with ink and pen,
To cheat Pat on the railway.
Chorus:

4. It's "Pat, do this," and "Pat, do that,"
Without a stocking or cravat,
And nothing but an old straw hat,
While Pat works on the railway.
Chorus:

5. And when Pat lays him down to sleep,
The wiry bugs around him creep,
An' Divil a bit can poor Pat sleep,
While he works on the railway.
Chorus:

6. In eighteen hundred and forty-three
'Twas then I met sweet Biddy McGee,
An illygant wife she's been to me,
While workin' on the railway.
Chorus:

7. In eighteen hundred and forty-six,
The gang pelted me with stones and bricks,
Oh, I was in a hell of a fix,
While workin' on the railway.
Chorus:

8. In eighteen hundred forty-seven,
Sweet Biddy McGee she went to heaven,
If she left one child, she left eleven
To work upon the railway.
Chorus:

9. In eighteen hundred and forty-eight,
I learned to take my whiskey straight,
'Tis an illygant drink and can't be bate,
For workin' on the railway.

CHORUS

Fil-li-me-oo-re-i-re-ay,
Fil-li-me-oo-re-i-re-ay,
Fil-li-me-oo-re-i-re-ay,
To work upon the railway.

BLOW THE MAN DOWN

Probably the most famous of the halyard shanties. The old melody rarely varies but there are many different versions of the words.

With rolling rhythm

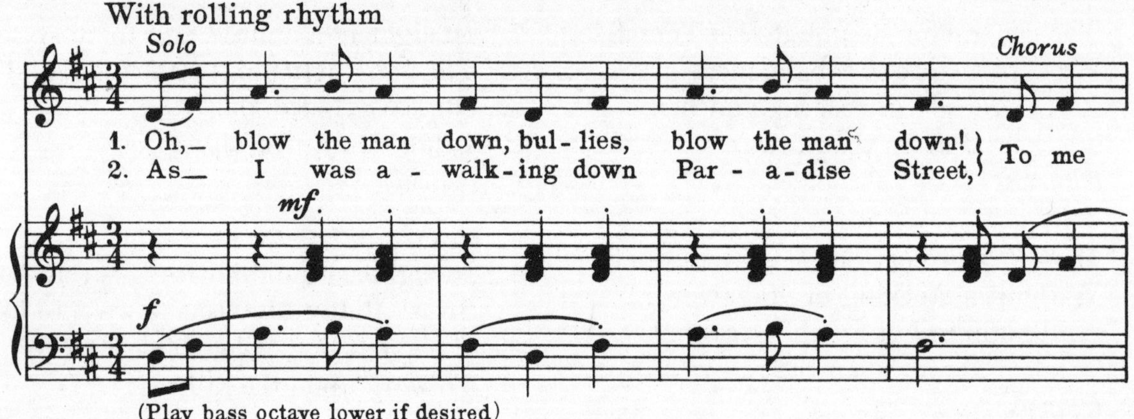

Solo
Chorus
1. Oh, blow the man down, bul-lies, blow the man down!
2. As I was a-walk-ing down Par-a-dise Street,
To me
mf
f

(Play bass octave lower if desired)

Solo
way - aye blow the man down.
Oh, blow the man down, bul-lies,
A pret-ty young dam-sel I

Chorus
blow him a - way.
chanced for to meet.
Give me some time to blow the man down!
Ped.
Ped.
Ped.
Ped.

3. She was round in the counter and bluff in the bow,
Chorus: To me way-aye, blow the man down.
So I took in all sail and cried, "Way enough now."
Chorus: Give me some time to blow the man down!

4. So I tailed her my flipper and took her in tow,
Chorus: To me way-aye, blow the man down.
And yardarm to yardarm away we did go.
Chorus: Give me some time to blow the man down!

5. But as we were going she said unto me,
Chorus: To me way-aye, blow the man down.
"There's a spanking full-rigger just ready for sea."
Chorus: Give me some time to blow the man down!

6. But as soon as that packet was clear of the bar,
Chorus: To me way-aye, blow the man down.
The mate knocked me down with the end of a spar.
Chorus: Give me some time to blow the man down!

7. So I give you fair warning before we belay,
Chorus: To me way-aye, blow the man down.
Don't never take heed of what pretty girls say.
Chorus: Give me some time to blow the man down!

BOSTON COME-ALL-YE

(or THE FISHES)

With a swagger
mf Solo
1. Come all ye young sail - or - men, lis - ten to me,— I'll
2. Oh first come the whale the big - gest of all,— He
sing you a song of the fish of the sea.
climb up a - loft and let ev - ry sail fall.
f Chorus
Then

A forecastle song. This very popular and imaginative song began life with the fishing fleet. The chorus is very like the Scottish fishing song, "Blaw the Wind Southerly."

blow ye winds west - er - ly, west - er - ly blow, We're
bound to the south - ward, so stead - y she goes.

3. And next come the mack'rel with his striped back;
He hauled aft the sheets and boarded each tack.
Chorus:

4. Then come the porpoise with his short snout;
He went to the wheel, calling, "Ready! About!"
Chorus:

5. Then come the smelt, the smallest of all;
He jumped to the poop and sung out, "Topsail, haul!"
Chorus:

6. The herring came saying, "I'm king of the seas,
If you want any wind, I'll blow you a breeze."
Chorus:

7. Next come the cod with his chuckle-head;
He went to the main-chains to heave at the lead.
Chorus:

8. Last come the flounder as flat as the ground;
Says, "Damn your eyes, chuckle-head, mind how you sound."
Chorus:

CHORUS

Then blow ye winds westerly, westerly blow,
We're bound to the southward, so steady she goes!

She'll Be Comin' Round the Mountain

An old-time Negro spiritual, "When the Chariot Comes," was made by mountaineers into "She'll Be Comin' Round the Mountain." The song spread to railroad work gangs in the west in the 1890's.

Boisterously
mf
1. She'll be com - in' round the moun-tain when she comes,
2. She'll be driv - in' six white hors - es when she comes,
mf
Ped.

She'll be com - in' round the moun-tain when she comes,
She'll be driv - in' six white hors - es when she comes,

She'll be com - in' round the moun-tain, She'll be com - in' round the
She'll be driv - in' six white hors - es, She'll be driv - in' six white

moun-tain, She'll be com - in' round the moun-tain when she comes.
hors - es, She'll be driv - in' six white hors - es when she comes.

Ped. Ped. Ped. Ped. Ped.

3. Oh, we'll all go to meet her when she comes,
Oh, we'll all go to meet her when she comes,
Oh, we'll all go to meet her,
Oh, we'll all go to meet her,
Oh, we'll all go to meet her when she comes.

4. We'll be singin' "Hallelujah" when she comes,
We'll be singin' "Hallelujah" when she comes,
We'll be singin' "Hallelujah,"
We'll be singin' "Hallelujah,"
We'll be singin' "Hallelujah" when she comes

ONE MORE DAY

A capstan shanty. This is a beautiful example of the "homeward-bound" shanty, a type well loved by the sailors. It is probably of Negro origin.

Moderato
mf Solo
Chorus
1. Oh have you heard the news, my John-ny?
2. Oh heave and sight the an-chor, John-ny,
3. I'm bound a-way to leave you, John-ny,
One more day!
mf
Solo
Chorus
We're home-ward bound to-mor-row,
Oh heave and sight the an-chor,
But I will not de-ceive you,
One more
Ped.

Chorus
day! On - ly one more day, my John - ny, One more_
day! Oh rock and row me o - ver, One more_ day.

Can't You Dance the Polka?

A capstan shanty. The tune of this shanty is "Larry Doolan," a shore ballad. The shanty dates from the last days of the packet ships when American sailors had already begun to cut their hair "short behind" in modern fashion.

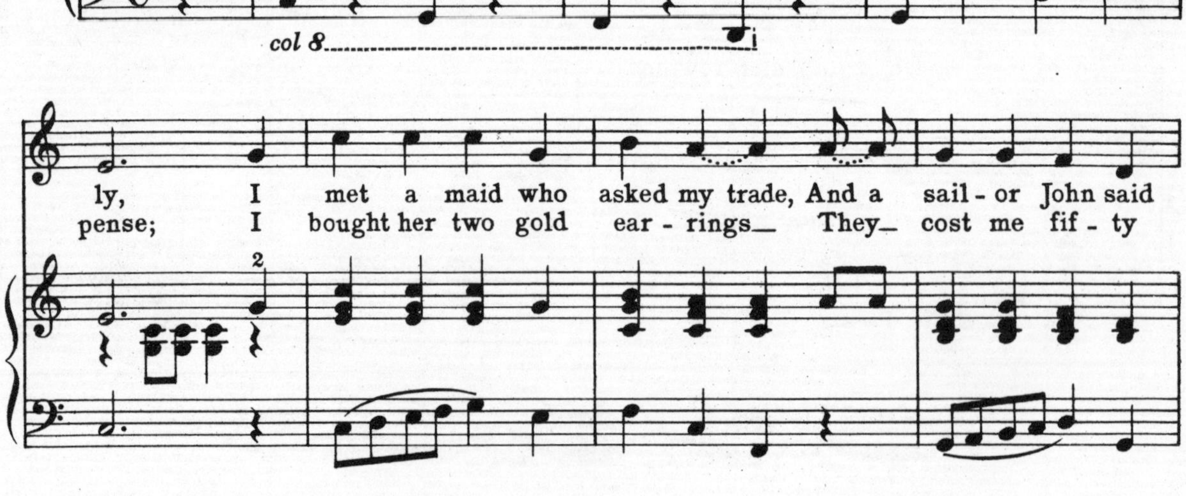
Gaily
mf Solo
1. As I came down the Bow-ery, One eve-ning in Ju - ly, I met a maid who asked my trade, And a sail-or John said
2. To Tif-fan-ny's I took her, I did not mind ex - pense; I bought her two gold ear-rings— They— cost me fif-ty
mf
col 8
2

Chorus
I ___ cents, Then a - way, you Sant - y my dear An-nie,
Oh, you New York girls, can't you dance the pol - ka?
8va bass

3. Says she, "You lime-juice sailor,
Now see me home you may,"
But when we reached her cottage door
She unto me did say:
Chorus:

4. "My young man he's a sailor,
With his hair cut short behind;
He wears a tarry jumper,
And he sails in the Black Ball line."
Chorus:

CHORUS

Then away, you Santy, my dear Annie,
Oh, you New York girls, can't you dance the polka?

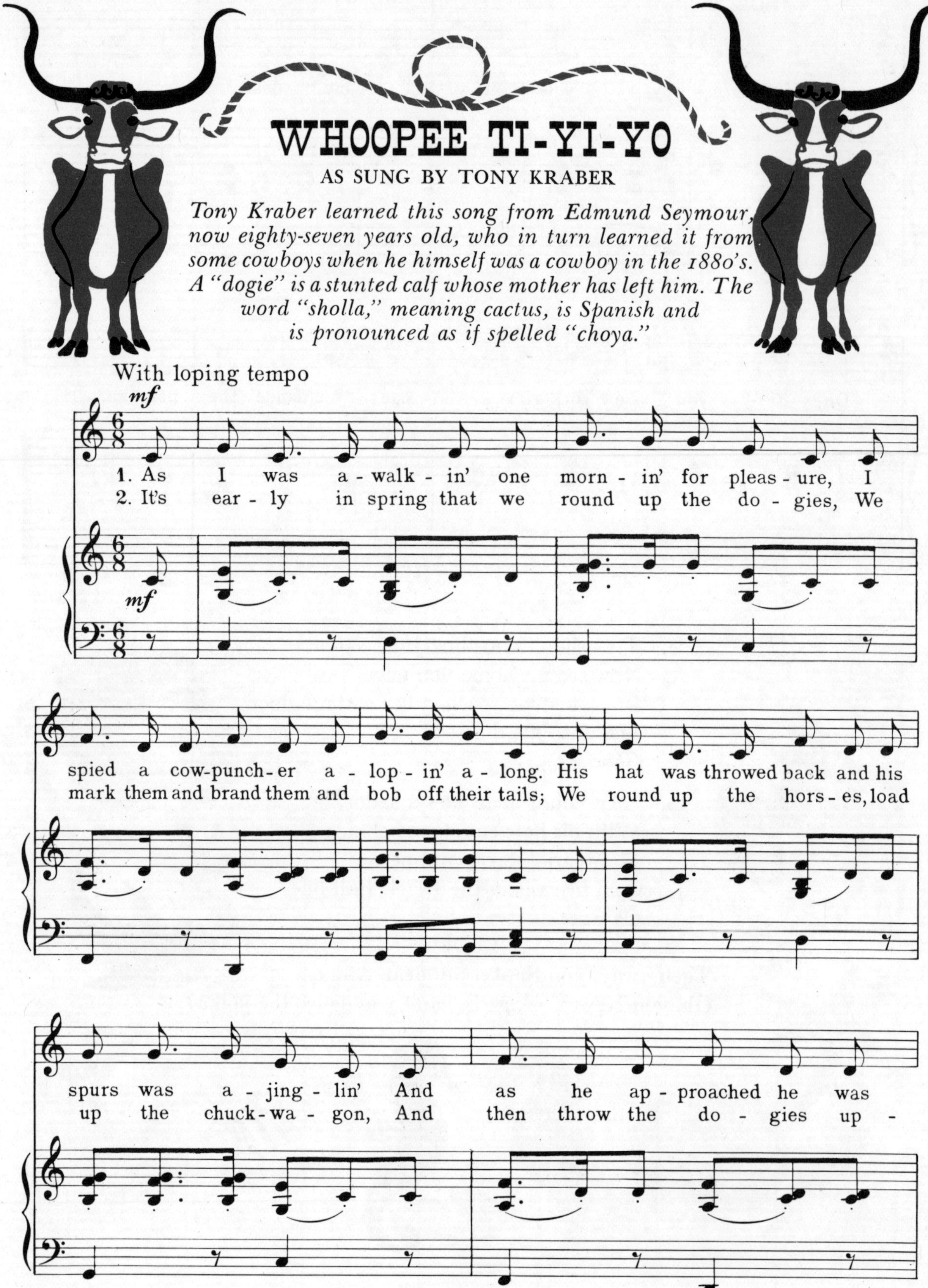
WHOOPEE TI-YI-YO
AS SUNG BY TONY KRABER
Tony Kraber learned this song from Edmund Seymour, now eighty-seven years old, who in turn learned it from some cowboys when he himself was a cowboy in the 1880's. A "dogie" is a stunted calf whose mother has left him. The word "sholla," meaning cactus, is Spanish and is pronounced as if spelled "choya."
With loping tempo
mf
1. As I was a - walk - in' one morn - in' for pleas - ure, I
2. It's ear - ly in spring that we round up the do - gies, We
mf
spied a cow-punch-er a - lop - in' a - long. His hat was throwed back and his
mark them and brand them and bob off their tails; We round up the hors - es, load
spurs was a - jing - lin' And as he ap - proached he was
up the chuck - wa - gon, And then throw the do - gies up -

f Chorus

sing - in' this song: / on the long trail. } Whoo-pee ti - yi - yo, git a - long lit - tle do-gies, For you

know that Wy - o - ming 'll be your new home. Whoo-pee, ti - yi - yo, git a -

long lit - tle do - gies, For you know that Wy - o - ming 'll be your new home.

3. Your mother was raised away down in Texas,
Where the jimpson weed and sand-burrs grow,
Now we'll fill you up on prickly pear and cholla,
Till you are all ready for the trail to Idaho.
Chorus:

4. Oh, you'll be soup for Uncle Sam's Injuns,
"It's beef, heap beef!" I hear them cry.
Git along, git along, git along little dogies,
You'll be beef steers by and by.
Chorus:

HOME ON THE RANGE

This song, according to John Lomax, was first printed in 1911, and for twenty years attracted practically no attention. It is said to have been sung on the doorstep of Franklin D. Roosevelt's home by a group of newspaper reporters the night he was first elected President.

Moderato
mf
1. Oh, give me a home, where the buf - fa - lo roam, Where the
2. How of - ten at night when the heav - ens are bright With the
mf
deer and the an - te-lope play;
lights from the glit - ter-ing stars;
Where sel - dom is heard a dis-
Have I stood there a-mazed and
cour - ag-ing word, And the skies are not cloud - y all day.
asked as I gazed If their glo - ry ex-ceeds that of ours.

Chorus
Home, home on the range,— Where the deer and the an-te-lope play;— Where
sel-dom is heard a dis-cour-ag-ing word, And the skies are not cloud-y all day.—

3. Oh, give me a land where the bright diamond sand
Flows leisurely down the stream;
Where the graceful, white swan goes gliding along,
Like a maid in a heavenly dream.
Chorus:

4. Where the air is so pure, the zephyrs so free,
The breezes so balmy and light,
That I would not exchange my home on the range
For all of the cities so bright.
Chorus:

5. Oh, I love those wild flowers in this dear land of ours,
The curlew I love to hear scream,
And I love the white rocks and the antelope flocks
That graze on the mountain tops green.
Chorus:

CHORUS

Home, home on the range,
Where the deer and the antelope play;
Where seldom is heard a discouraging word,
And the skies are not cloudy all day.

THE COASTS OF HIGH BARBARY

How old this song is no one can tell. It appears in Francis James Child's The English and Scottish Ballads *as "The George Aloe and the Sweepstake," and tells of an early fight between the French and the English. The revival of the song probably dates back to the period between 1795 and 1815, a period when pirates were taking a heavy toll of commerce.*

Vigorously
f Solo
1. Look a - head, look a - stern, look the weath - er in the lee.
2. "O are you a pi - rate or man - o - war?" cried we.
f
with pedal
Chorus
Blow high! Blow low! and so sail - ed we.
Solo
I
"O

Chorus
see a wreck to wind-ward and_ a loft-y ship to lee,
no! I'm not a pi-rate but_ a man-o-war," cried he,
A
sail-ing down all on the coasts of High Bar-bar-y.

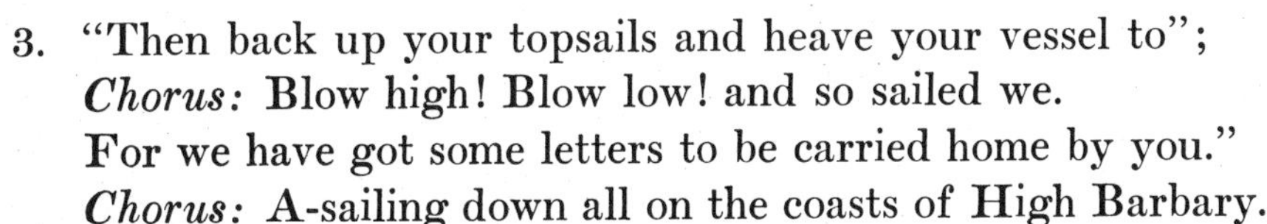
3. "Then back up your topsails and heave your vessel to";
Chorus: Blow high! Blow low! and so sailed we.
For we have got some letters to be carried home by you."
Chorus: A-sailing down all on the coasts of High Barbary.

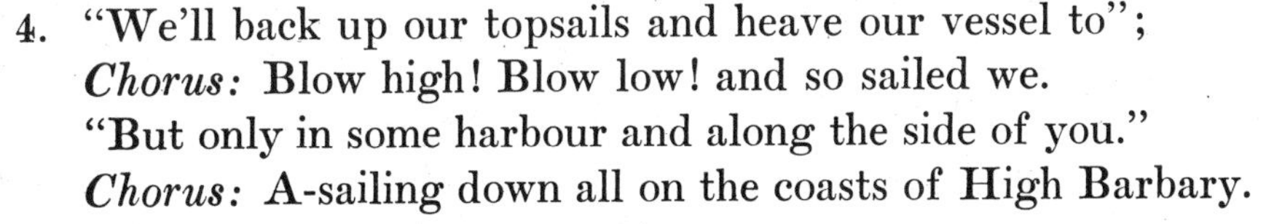
4. "We'll back up our topsails and heave our vessel to";
Chorus: Blow high! Blow low! and so sailed we.
"But only in some harbour and along the side of you."
Chorus: A-sailing down all on the coasts of High Barbary.

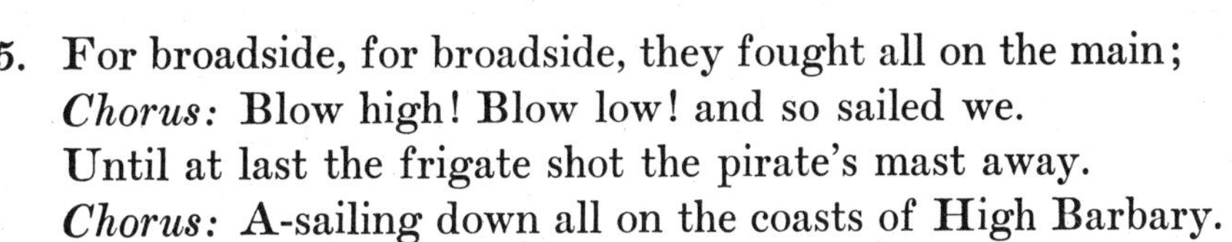
5. For broadside, for broadside, they fought all on the main;
Chorus: Blow high! Blow low! and so sailed we.
Until at last the frigate shot the pirate's mast away.
Chorus: A-sailing down all on the coasts of High Barbary.

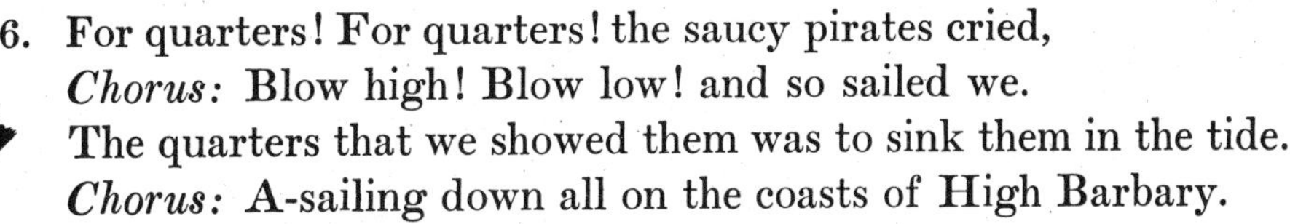
6. For quarters! For quarters! the saucy pirates cried,
Chorus: Blow high! Blow low! and so sailed we.
The quarters that we showed them was to sink them in the tide.
Chorus: A-sailing down all on the coasts of High Barbary.

7. With cutlass and gun, O we fought for hours three;
Chorus: Blow high! Blow low! and so sailed we.
The ship it was their coffin, and their grave it was the sea.
Chorus: A-sailing down all on the coasts of High Barbary.

A-ROVING
One of the oldest of the capstan shanties.
Originally a shore song.
Lively
mf Solo
Chorus
1. In Ply-mouth town there liv'd a maid,
2. I took this fair maid for a walk,
Bless you young
mf
Solo
Chorus
poco rit.
3
wo - men; In Ply-mouth town there liv'd a maid,
I took this fair maid for a walk,
O mind what I do
3
poco rit.
3
Solo
a tempo
say, In Ply-mouth town there liv'd a maid, And she was mis - tress
I took this fair maid for a walk, And we had such a
a tempo

poco rit.
Chorus
f a tempo
of her trade; I'll go no more a - rov - ing with you, fair
lov - ing talk.
a tempo
poco rit.
f
Ped.
maid.
f Chorus
A - rov - ing, a - rov - ing, since rov-ing's been my
f
poco rit.
f a tempo
ru - i - in, I'll go no more a - rov - ing with you, fair maid.
f
Ped.

3. O didn't I tell her stories too,
Chorus: Bless you, young women;
O didn't I tell her stories too,
Chorus: O mind what I do say.
O didn't I tell her whoppers too
Of the gold I found in Timbuctoo,

CHORUS

I'll go no more a-roving with you, fair maid.
A-roving, a-roving, since roving's been my ru-i-in,
I'll go no more a-roving with you, fair maid.

JOHN HENRY

One of the many legends about John Henry, famous steel driller of West Virginia around 1870, tells how he laid down his life to convince himself and others that he could beat a machine. A contest was arranged by two companies in Big Bend Tunnel: John Henry against a steam drill,—"de flesh ag'in de steam." "De flesh" won, but John Henry broke a blood vessel and died.

Heavily

f

1. John_ Hen - ry said_ to_ his cap - tain,_ "A_ man ain't noth - ing but a man. An' be - fore I'll let your steam drill
2. John_ Hen - ry got a thir - ty pound ham - mer,_ Be - side the steam drill he did stand. He_ beat_ that steam_ drill

etc.

beat me down, Die — with the ham - mer in my
three in - ches down, An' died — with his ham - mer in his
hand, Lawd, Lawd! Die — with the ham-mer in my hand."
hand, Lawd, Lawd! Died — with his ham-mer in his hand.

3. John Henry had a little woman
An' she was always dressed in blue,
She went down track never looking back,
Says, "John Henry, I am always true to you, Lawd, Lawd!
John Henry, I am always true to you."

4. "Who gonna shoe your pretty feet,
Who gonna comb your bangs?
Who gonna kiss your rose-red lips,
Who gonna be your man, Lawd, Lawd!
Who gonna be your man?"

5. "Sweet Papa gonna shoe your pretty feet,
Sister gonna comb your bangs,
Mama gonna kiss your rose-red lips,
John Henry gonna be your man, Lawd, Lawd!
John Henry gonna be your man."

6. John Henry had a pretty little boy,
Sittin' in the palm of his hand.
He hugged and kissed him an' bid him farewell,
"Oh son, do the best you can, Lawd, Lawd!
Son, do the best you can."

7. They took John Henry to the graveyard
An' they buried him in the sand,
An' ev'ry locomotive come roarin' by
Says, "Dere lays a steel-drivin' man, Lawd, Lawd!
Dere lays a steel-drivin' man."

THE GOLDEN VANITY
An English folk song which was sung
as a forecastle shanty
Not too fast, but with vigor
mf
1. There was a ship came_ from the north coun-try, And the
2. Then up there came a___ lit - tle ca - bin boy, And he
name of the ship was the Gold - en Van - i - ty, And they
said to the skip - per, "What will you give to me, If I
broaden
a tempo
feared she might be ta - ken by the Turk - ish e - ne - my, That sails up - on the Low - land,
swim a - long - side_ of the Turk - ish e - ne - my, And sink her in the Low - land,
f
broaden
mf

poco rit.
a tempo
Low - land, Low - land, That sails up - on the Low - land sea.
Low - land, Low - land, And sink her in the Low - land sea?"
poco rit.
a tempo

3. "O, I will give you silver and I will give you gold,
And my only daughter your bride to be,
If you'll swim alongside of the Turkish enemy,
And sink her in the Lowland, Lowland, Lowland,
And sink her in the Lowland sea.

4. Then the boy made him ready, and overboard sprang he,
And he swam alongside of the Turkish enemy,
And with his auger sharp in her side he bored holes three,
And he sank her in the Lowland, Lowland, Lowland,
And he sank her in the Lowland sea.

5. Then the boy turned round, and back again swam he,
And he cried out to the skipper of the Golden Vanity;
But the skipper did not heed, for his promise he would need;
And he left him in the Lowland, Lowland, Lowland,
And he left him in the Lowland sea.

6. Then the boy swam round, and came to the port side,
And he looked up at his messmates, and bitterly he cried;
"O messmates, take me up, for I'm drifting with the tide
And I'm sinking in the Lowland, Lowland, Lowland,
I'm sinking in the Lowland sea!"

7. Then his messmates took him up, but on the deck he died;
And they sewed him in his hammock that was so large and wide;
And they lowered him overboard, but he drifted with the tide,
And he sank beneath the Lowland, Lowland, Lowland,
He sank beneath the Lowland sea!

Green Grow the Lilacs

(AS SUNG BY TONY KRABER)

An old Irish song, widely popular with the early Texas cowboys. A colorful fable holds that the Mexican word "gringo," meaning cowboy, was derived from the song, for the Mexicans referred to the Americans by the first two words of the title "Green Grow," pronouncing it "Gringo."

Quite simply
mp
1. Green grow___ the li - lacs, all spark-ling with dew, I'm
2. I used to have a sweet-heart, but now I have none, Since
mp
Ped. Ped. Ped. Ped.
lone - ly, my dar - ling, since part - ing with you. But
she's gone and left me, I care not for one. Since
Ped. Ped. Ped. Ped. ✻ Ped.

by our next meet - ing I'll hope to prove true, And
she's gone and left me, con - tent - ed I'll be, For
change the green li - lacs to the Red, White and Blue.
she loves an - oth - er one___ bet - ter than me.

3. I passed my love's window, both early and late,
The look that she gave me, it made my heart ache.
Oh, the look that she gave me was painful to see,
For she loves another one better than me.

4. I wrote my love letters in rosy red lines,
She sent me an answer all twisted in twines,
Saying, "Keep your love letters and I will keep mine,
Just you write to your love and I'll write to mine."

5. Green grow the lilacs, all sparkling with dew,
I'm lonely, my darling, since parting with you,
But by our next meeting I'll hope to prove true,
And change the green lilacs to Red, White and Blue.

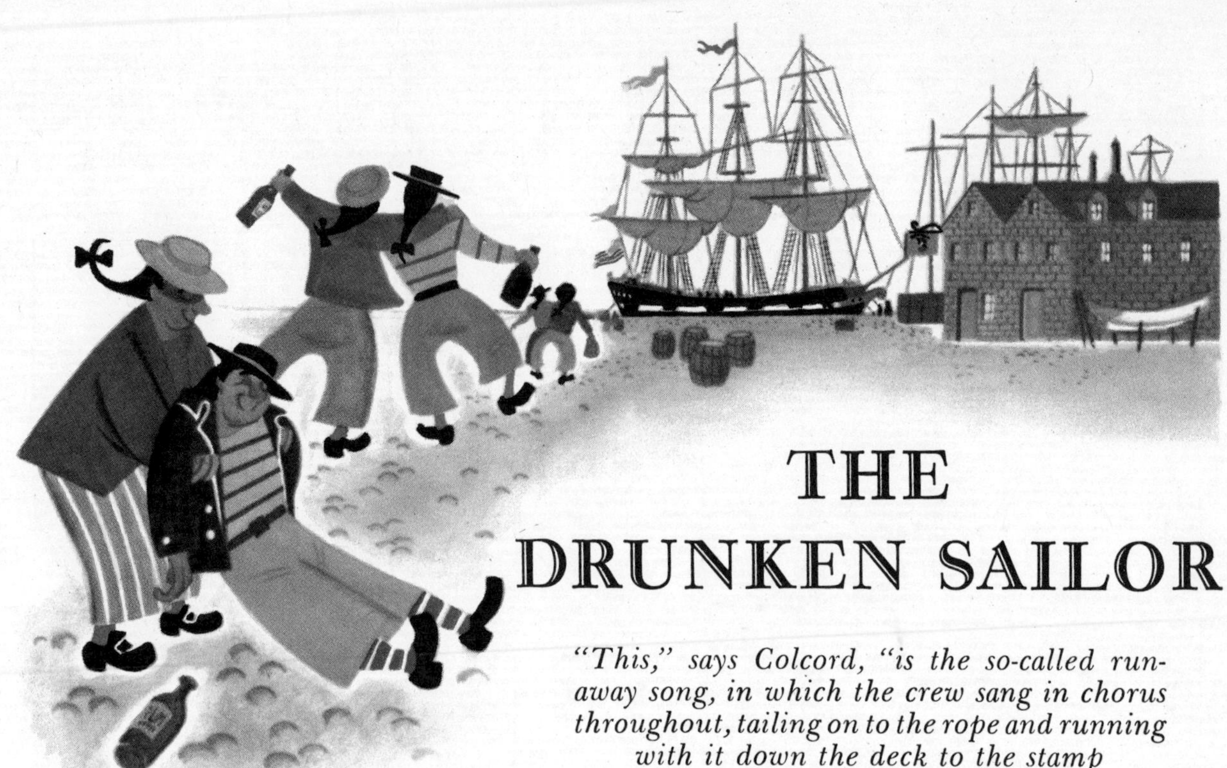

THE DRUNKEN SAILOR

"This," says Colcord, "is the so-called runaway song, in which the crew sang in chorus throughout, tailing on to the rope and running with it down the deck to the stamp and go of the music."

With gusto

mf *Solo*

1. What shall we do— with the drunk-en sail-or, What shall we do— with the
2. Put him in the long - boat— till he's so-ber, Put him in the long - boat—

mf

drunk-en sail - or, What— shall we do— with the drunk-en sail - or,
till he's so - ber, Put him in the long - boat— till he's so - ber,

Chorus
Ear-lye in the morn-ing. Hoo - ray and up she ri - ses, Hoo - ray and
up she ri - ses, Hoo - ray and up she ri - ses, Ear-lye in the morn-ing.

3. Pull out the plug and wet him all over,
   Pull out the plug and wet him all over,
   Pull out the plug and wet him all over,
   Earlye in the morning.
   Chorus:

4. Put him in the scuppers with a hose-pipe on him,
   Put him in the scuppers with a hose-pipe on him,
   Put him in the scuppers with a hose-pipe on him,
   Earlye in the morning.
   Chorus:

5. Heave him by the leg in a running bow-lin',
   Heave him by the leg in a running bow-lin',
   Heave him by the leg in a running bow-lin',
   Earlye in the morning.
   Chorus:

CHORUS

Hoo-ray and up she rises,
Hoo-ray and up she rises,
Hoo-ray and up she rises,
Earlye in the morning.

MARCHING SONGS AND SONGS OF VALOR

PRO PATRIA

Marching Songs and Songs of Valor

IN THE PAST, ironically enough, one of the more potent forms of song has been produced by war. Good fighting songs have been written in almost every century and every country. Some of them came spontaneously from the soldiers themselves; some were written by noncombatants in a deliberate attempt to whip up patriotism and fighting fervor. Only the best of them are still remembered—but these have a curious power to stir, although the wars they celebrated have long been forgotten.

It is a little difficult to determine just what quality makes these songs of valor moving. Probably the secret of their appeal is that they were preserved by the most selective of audiences—the soldiers themselves. Fighting men are less stirred by the "glamour" of battle than are civilians, and any song which is acceptable to them must have a singular power, and generally be free from sentimentality about war. There is something—a melody truly and movingly martial, or a lyric exciting in its passion—that makes them cling affectionately to a nation's memory, and they endure to outlive their military purposes, and to be sung by school children, by group choruses, or by individuals humming an absent-minded tune.

It is perhaps significant that among the songs of the most recent world conflict those which seem most slated to live are the guerrilla songs—songs produced in the Spanish Civil War, in China and in Russia, songs just beginning to make themselves heard from the Norwegian, French, and Czechoslovakian undergrounds and the other bands of partisans. Even such underground songs were limited by the physical conditions of the fighting. There is a story told—possibly apocryphal—of an American composer who went into France shortly after its liberation, searching for the music of the Maquis. Meeting a French underground leader one evening, he questioned him as to the melodies and lyrics of the French resistance. The leader smiled at him. "I'm afraid you won't find much in the way of music," he said. "Why?" the American composer asked. "Because," said the Frenchman looking around dramatically and then lowering his voice to a whisper, "you see, we always had to talk like this!"

But if the underground songs were limited, at least the few that have been written are popular with men of any nation. As for the uniformed soldiers of this past war, they seemed to produce few fighting songs of any great merit or appeal. The most popular soldier's melody was the wholly sentimental homefront song "Lili Marlene," which was adopted by soldiers and civilians more wholeheartedly than any other. The song began in Germany in 1938 and was credited to a composer named Norbert Schultze. It was not particularly well liked until war broke out and German technicians on Radio Belgrade used the record to sign off their programs. German troops listening from far fronts to the powerful radio station began pouring in requests for more and more performances of the song. Its sweet sentimental strains were heard nightly . . . its singer, Lala Andersen, began to receive masses of fan mail . . . Frau Goering undertook to sing it at Berlin's Kroll Opera House. The song was a runaway success. Its response would have been swelled even more enormously if the Germans had heard from another large soldier audience who listened to it. In the Libyan desert, the British Eighth Army heard Radio Belgrade and blithely adopted "Lili Marlene" for their own. They changed the words to suit their own tastes, and there were a variety of parodies, usually profane ones. But the sentimental tune sang them to sleep at night, and they carried it on with them throughout the whole Italian campaign. The song grew. The Australians, New Zealanders, and South Africans, as well as Englishmen, of the British Eighth Army took it back to their far homes. American troops fighting at Anzio picked it up, and it became theirs too. The Italian people, hearing the soldier song, gave it their own emotional words, and every little child on the street learned to sing it. The versions grew and grew; the words never mattered, it was the soft melody which had a peculiar magic for the fighting men, and their brothers in the underground also succumbed to its charms. Parody versions sprang up in Denmark and Norway, and the "lamppost" of the song, which in the German version illuminated a young soldier and his girl, was used in a manner more significant in the occupied countries—usually a little man with rumpled hair hung from it. There is no rhyme or reason for the popularity of "Lili Marlene," but there it is. And certainly the most universally accepted of all soldier songs should be included in this section on Songs of Valor.

As for marching songs, the uniformed troops of this war did not take to them. This was a thoroughly mechanized war, and troops transported in swiftly moving trucks or trains need no rhythmic accompaniment. Almost every man, except in the thick of the fighting itself, had access to a radio, and his songs were brought to him—songs of home and the people at home, which after all more completely absorbed him than anything else. As for songs of valor, it would seem that they belong to other times, and only the anachronism of guerrilla fighting, with its personal and often romantic nature, produced them in World War II. Perhaps in the future the songs men sing in praise of valor will celebrate the efforts and victories not of war but of peace. Wars themselves have ceased to be a singing matter.

LIBERTY

THE STAR SPANGLED BANNER

Our national anthem was written by Francis Scott Key during the attack of the British on Fort McHenry, September 13, 1814. Key had gone out from Baltimore to the British fleet to obtain the release of a friend, held prisoner. He arrived on the eve of the bombardment of the city by the British, and was detained on his own vessel lest the plans of the attack be disclosed. All day and night he watched the battle anxiously from the deck. When morning dawned and showed the Stars and Stripes still floating over the Fort, he was deeply moved and quickly wrote the words of the poem. They were later set to the tune of an old English drinking song, "Anacreon in Heaven," a song widely sung in this country at that time.

Words by Francis Scott Key

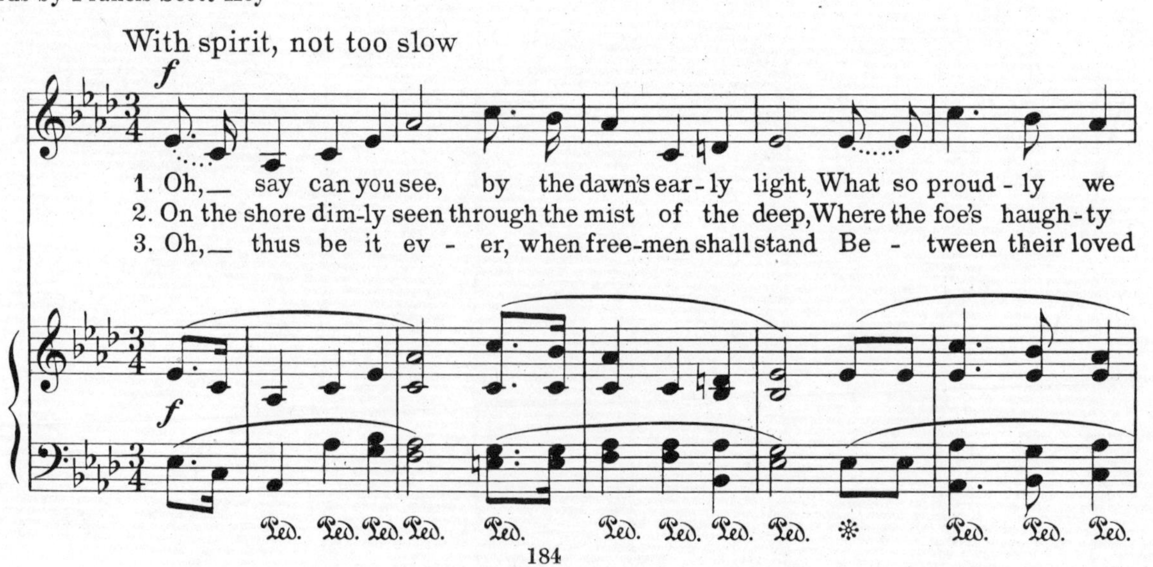
With spirit, not too slow
f
1. Oh,— say can you see, by the dawn's ear-ly light, What so proud-ly we
2. On the shore dim-ly seen through the mist of the deep, Where the foe's haugh-ty
3. Oh,— thus be it ev - er, when free-men shall stand Be - tween their loved
f

hailed at the twi-light's last gleam-ing? Whose broad stripes and bright stars, thro' the
host in dread si - lence re - pos - es, What is that which the breeze, o'er the
homes and the war's des - o - la - tion, Blessed with vic - t'ry and peace, may the

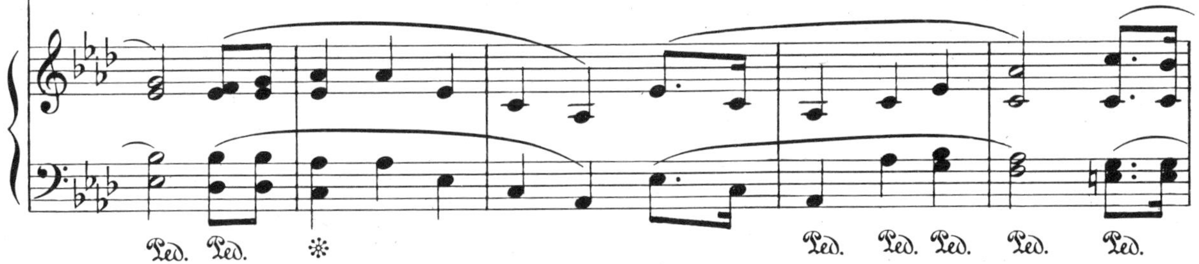

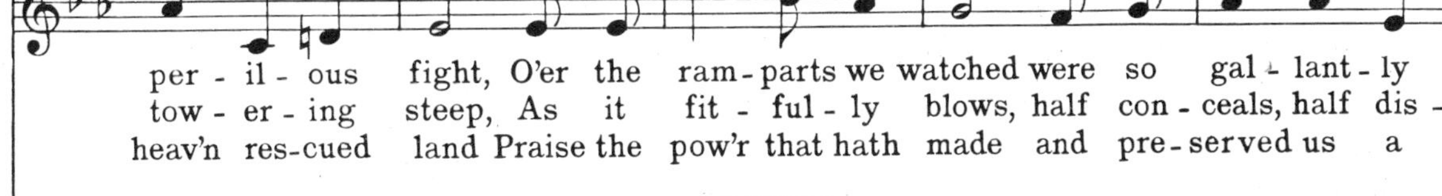
per - il - ous fight, O'er the ram - parts we watched were so gal - lant - ly
tow - er - ing steep, As it fit - ful - ly blows, half con - ceals, half dis -
heav'n res-cued land Praise the pow'r that hath made and pre - served us a

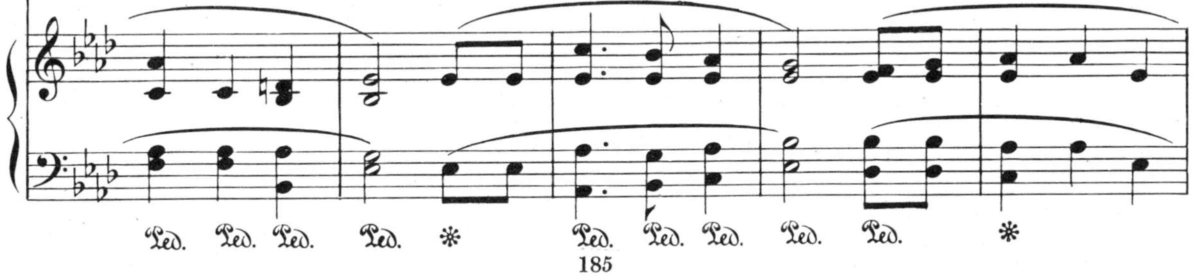

streaming? And the rock-et's red glare, the bombs burst-ing in air, Gave
clos - es? Now it catch-es the gleam of the morn-ing's first beam, In full
na - tion. Then conquer we must, when our cause it is just, And
Chorus
proof thro' the night that our flag was still there. Oh say does that star-span-gled
glo - ry re-flect-ed, now shines on the stream; 'Tis the star-span-gled ban-ner! Oh
this be our mot-to, "In God is our trust!" And the star-span-gled ban-ner in
poco rit.
broader
ban - ner yet wave O'er the land of the free and the home of the brave?
long may it wave O'er the land of the free and the home of the brave!
tri - umph shall wave O'er the land of the free and the home of the brave!
poco rit.
broader

MANY THOUSAN' GONE

"A song to which the rebellion has actually given rise. This was composed by nobody knows whom . . . and has been sung in secret. The peck of corn and the pint of salt were slavery rations." (W. P. Allen: *Slave Songs of the United States*)

With dignity

mf

1. No mo' auc - tion block for me, No mo', no mo',
2. No mo' driv - er's lash for me, No mo', no mo',
3. No mo' pint o' salt for me, No mo', no mo',

No mo' auc - tion block for me, Man - y thou - san' gone.
No mo' driv - er's lash for me, Man - y thou - san' gone.
No mo' pint o' salt for me, Man - y thou - san' gone.

col 8

Marche Lorraine

The modern, martial version of this ancient French folk song was made familiar to American GI's in North Africa by the Free French units there, and in August, 1944, LeClerc's units, spearheading the Allied drive into Paris, entered the City of Light chanting its heroic strains. Its use was suggested by the symbol of the Free French movement, the Cross of Lorraine.

Words by Jules Jouy and Octave Pradels
Translation by Phyllis Mead

Music by Louis Ganne

Lively

mf

1. Come on, you lads of old Lor-raine, Lift the song once a-gain, And
2. And when they marched a - way to war, Joan of Arc rode be-fore. She
3. The sons of France are just as bold, Just as brave as of old; The

join in the prais-es we bring to her, The Vir-gin of Mo - selle.— Come
car-ried the ban-ner we love so well, The cross of old Lor - raine.— Then
blood in their veins is the same to-day, The blood of La Pu - celle.— Our

on, my lads, and ga - ther 'round, Let the skies all re-sound, And
home they came vic - to - ri - ous, Home they came, glo - ri - ous; They
fa - thers went to meet the foe Man-y a time, long a - go, And

ech - o the song that we sing to her, ___ To the Maid of Mo-selle: Here's to
wak-ened the ech - oes a - bove to tell ___ They had con-quered a - gain: Here's to
we shall re-mem - ber their fame to-day, ___ And the song of Mo-selle: Like the
Joan of old Lor - raine, The maid in wood - en shoes, ___ She who
Joan of old Lor - raine, Who left her wood - en shoes; ___ When she
Maid of old Lor - raine, We've on - ly wood - en shoes. ___ In the
heard the call of dan - ger, And did not re - fuse, ___ Left her
sum - moned us to dan - ger, We could not re - fuse. ___ Cap - tain
dark and in the dan - ger, What have we to lose? ___ Ev - 'ry
sheep up - on the plain, _ Went a - march-ing through Lor - raine, _ oh, oh,
Joan did not com - plain _ March-ing on in wind and rain, _ oh, oh,
gun is aimed and read - y Ev - 'ry hand is sure and stead - y, oh, oh,

sf
oh, March-ing through Lor - raine. See her march-ing a -
oh, March-ing through Lor - raine. What shall be her re -
oh, Fight-ing for Lor - raine. Hill and val-ley and
sf
Ped. Ped.
long, so val-iant and strong to pre-vail o - ver wrong!
ward who took up the sword in the cause of her Lord?
plain shall hear the re - frain as we march through Lor - raine!
ff
ff
mf Refrain
1.& 3. Come you chil - dren of Lor - raine, From the
2. Then at last she was for - sa - ken. Trai - tor's
mf
hills, o - ver the plain. Sons of France ral - ly like men!
hands let her be ta - ken, Heart-less foes led her to doom,
Ped. Ped.

— Joan of Arc is calling a - gain.
— To the fire, her on - ly tomb?
mf
Men of Gaul, hear the com - mand.
Storms a -
Men of Gaul, fol - low the maid.
That bright
rise o - ver the land.
Men of Gaul, make your
flame nev - er will fade.
Good Saint Joan bless - es your
ff
stand! Wher - ev - er our foes ad - vance We'll fight for France!
blade. Wher - ev - er our foes ad - vance We'll fight for France!

DIXIE

Daniel Emmett wrote "Dixie" at the request of the manager of the famous Bryant minstrels for a new song to be used as a "walkaround" in their next stage show. It became immediately popular and was sung by various minstrel bands all over the country. When the Civil War started, the Southern soldiers claimed it for their marching song. Emmett, born in the North and of Union sympathies, was dismayed to have his song become a rallying song for the Southern cause and to find himself idolized by the South. In spite of the tremendous popularity of this and other songs of his, he died at the age of eighty-nine in complete poverty.

Words and Music by Daniel D. Emmett

Lively

mf

I— wish I was—in de land ob cot - ton, Old times dar am
In— Dix - ie Land whar— I was born in, Ear - ly on one

not for-got-ten, Look a - way! Look a - way! Look a - way! Dix-ie Land.
frost - y morn-in', Look a - way! Look a - way! Look a - way! Dix-ie Land.

Chorus

Den I wish I was in Dix-ie, Hoo-ray! Hoo-ray! In Dix-ie Land I'll

non legato

take my stand, To live and die in Dix-ie; A-way, a-way, a-

broader

way down south in Dix-ie, A-way, a-way, a-way down south in Dix-ie.

2. Dar's buckwheat cakes and Injun batter,
Makes you fat or a little fatter,
Look away! Look away! Look away! Dixie Land.
Den hoe it down and scratch your grabble,
To Dixie Land I'm bound to trabble,
Look away! Look away! Look away! Dixie Land.

CHORUS

Den I wish I was in Dixie,
Hooray! Hooray!
In Dixieland I'll take my stand,
To live and die in Dixie;
Away, away, away down south in Dixie,
Away, away, away down south in Dixie.

HATIKVAH

(THE HOPE)

"Hatikvah (The Hope)" was written in 1878 by the Hebrew poet Nephtali Herz Imber and was set to music by Samuel Cohen, one of the pioneer settlers in Rishon Le Zion, Palestine. The song was taken up by the Palestine colonists and became the anthem of the Zionist movement after it was organized in 1897. The melody is based on a Czechoslovakian folk song. (Sophia A. Udin, Director of the Zionist Archives and Library.)

Translation by Jacob Goodman

With determination

mf

As long_ as_ deep with - in_ the_heart The soul of Ju-de - a is

tur - bu-lent and strong, As long as to the East, for - ward-ly, The

eye to-ward Zi - on con-stant-ly is turned, Then our hope it is — not dead, The
an - cient long - ing will be — ful - filled, To re - turn to the land, — The
land — of our fa - thers, The cit - y of Je - ru - sa - lem, Where Da - vid en-camped.

WHEN JOHNNY COMES MARCHING HOME

Patrick Gilmore, a bandmaster of the Union Army, claimed that he heard this tune sung by a Negro and jotted it down. He, himself, was an Irishman, and it is far more likely that the tune is of Irish origin. The song has been a favorite with the army since its first singing.

Words and Music by Patrick S. Gilmore

Gaily
mf
1. When John-ny comes march-ing home a-gain, Hur-rah! Hur-rah! We'll give him a heart-y wel-come then, Hur-rah! Hur-
2. Get read-y for the Ju-bi-lee, Hur-rah! Hur-rah! We'll give the he-ro three times three, Hur-rah! Hur-

rah! The men will cheer the boys will shout, The lad-ies they will
rah! The lau-rel wreath is read-y now To place up-on his

all turn out, And we'll all feel gay When John-ny comes march-ing home.
loy-al brow, And we'll all feel gay When John-ny comes march-ing home.

3. In eighteen hundred and sixty-one,
Hurrah! Hurrah!
That was when the war begun,
Hurrah! Hurrah!
In eighteen hundred and sixty-two,
Both sides were falling to,
And we'll all drink stone wine,
When Johnny comes marching home.

4. In eighteen hundred and sixty-three,
Hurrah! Hurrah!
Abe Lincoln set the darkies free,
Hurrah! Hurrah!
In eighteen hundred and sixty-three
Old Abe set the darkies free,
And we'll all drink stone wine,
When Johnny comes marching home.

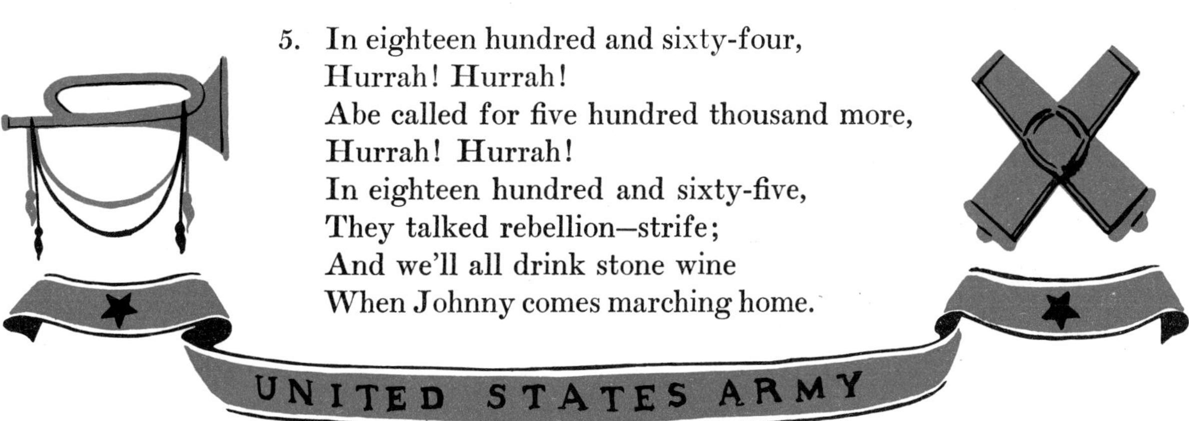
UNITED STATES ARMY

5. In eighteen hundred and sixty-four,
Hurrah! Hurrah!
Abe called for five hundred thousand more,
Hurrah! Hurrah!
In eighteen hundred and sixty-five,
They talked rebellion—strife;
And we'll all drink stone wine
When Johnny comes marching home.

THE BRITISH GRENADIERS

The origin of the tune is unknown, but it goes back to the sixteenth century. The words belong to a later period: the allusion to the use of hand grenades would place them at least toward the end of the seventeenth century. The tune has a spirit-stirring quality which is truly characteristic of English national music.

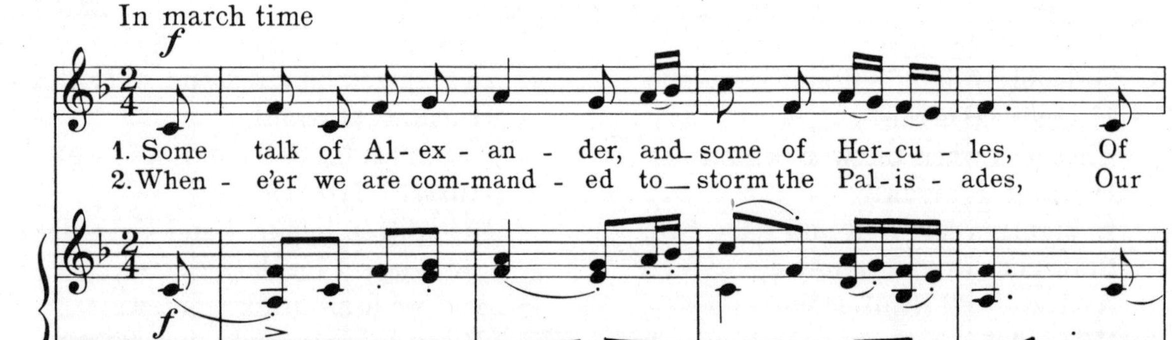

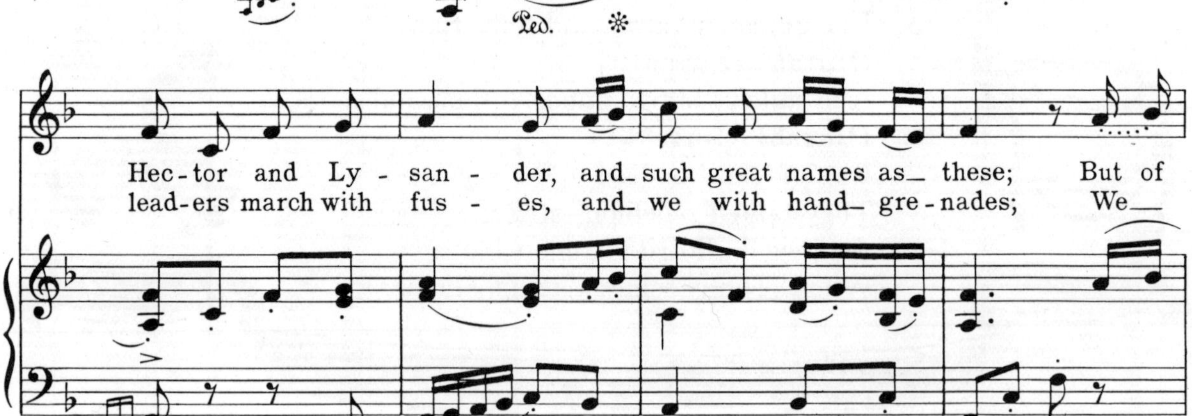

In march time

f

1. Some talk of Al-ex-an-der, and some of Her-cu-les, Of
2. When-e'er we are com-mand-ed to storm the Pal-is-ades, Our

Hec-tor and Ly-san-der, and such great names as these; But of
lead-ers march with fus-es, and we with hand gre-nades; We

all the world's brave he - roes there's none that can— com - pare,—With a
throw them from the gla - cis, a - bout the en-e-mies'— ears,—With a
tow, row, row, row, row, row, To the Bri-tish Gren-a - diers.
tow, row, row, row, row, row, The— Bri-tish Gren-a - diers.
Ped.

3. And when the siege is over, we to the town repair,
The townsmen cry, "Hurrah, boys, here comes a Grenadier;
Here come the Grenadiers, my boys, who know no doubts and fears!"
With a tow, etc.

4. Then let us fill a bumper, and drink the health of those
Who carry caps and pouches, and wear the loupéd clothes;
May they and their commanders live happy all their years,
With a tow, etc.

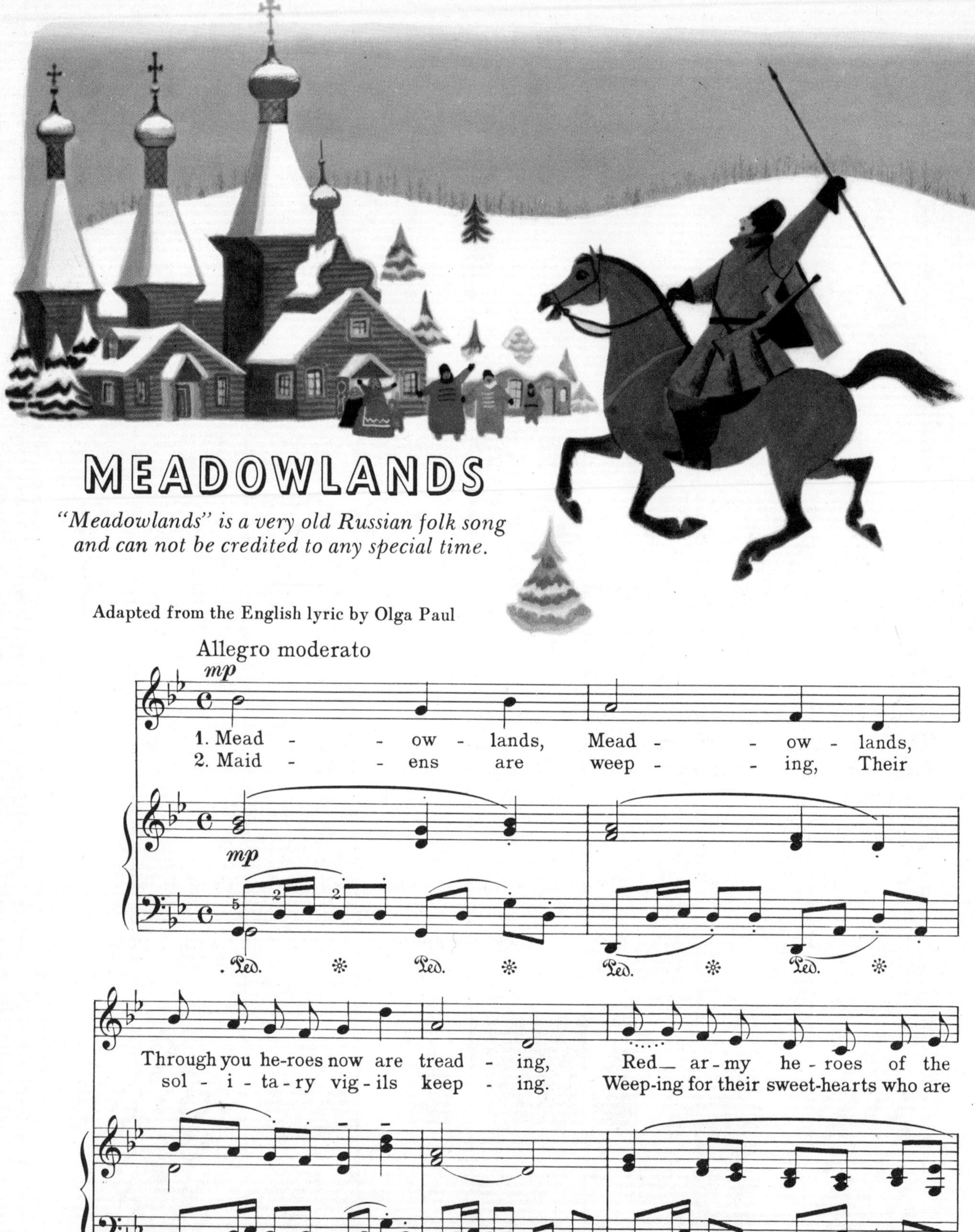
MEADOWLANDS
"Meadowlands" is a very old Russian folk song and can not be credited to any special time.
Adapted from the English lyric by Olga Paul
Allegro moderato
mp
1. Mead - - ow - lands, Mead - - ow - lands,
2. Maid - - ens are weep - - ing, Their
mp
Through you he-roes now are tread - ing, Red_ ar-my he - roes of the
sol - i - ta - ry vig - ils keep - ing. Weep-ing for their sweet-hearts who are

na - - tion, He-roes of the might-y Red Ar - my, Ah!
fight - - ing, Fight-ing in the might-y Red Ar - my. Ah!

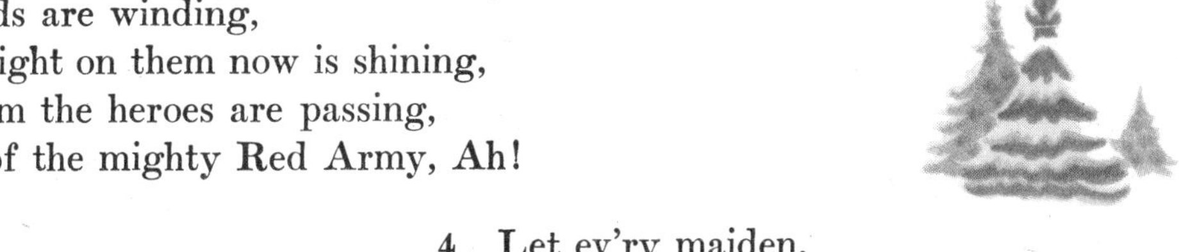

3. Gay roads are winding,
The sunlight on them now is shining,
Over them the heroes are passing,
Heroes of the mighty Red Army, Ah!

4. Let ev'ry maiden,
With heart no longer heavy laden,
Strike up the singing now more loudly,
Sing our fighting song so proudly, Ah!

LILI MARLENE

The music of "Lili Marlene," composed in Berlin in 1938, is credited to Norbert Schultze. The words were written in 1923 in Hamburg by the poet Hans Leip. The song, perhaps the most popular song of any time in German history, was "captured" by the British Eighth Army when they annihilated the German African Corps in the Libyan campaign, and through them presented to the outside world.

Sentimentally
mp
1. Un - der - neath the lan - tern by the bar - rack gate,
2. Time would come for roll - call, time for us to part,
mp
Dar - ling, I re - mem - ber the way you used to wait; 'Twas
Dar - ling, I'd ca - ress you and press you to my heart; And

poco rit. a tempo rit. a tempo rit. a tempo
there that you whis-pered ten - der - ly, That you lov'd me. You'd al - ways be My
there 'neath that far - off lan - tern light, I'd hold you tight. We'd kiss "Good-night," My
Li - li of the lamp - light, My own Li - li Mar - lene.
Li - li of the lamp - light, My own Li-li Mar - lene.
133

3. Orders came for sailing somewhere over there,
All confined to barracks was more than I could bear;
I knew you were waiting in the street,
I heard your feet,
But could not meet,
My Lili of the lamplight,
My own Lili Marlene.

4. Resting in a billet just behind the line,
Even tho' we're parted your lips are close to mine;
You wait where that lantern softly gleams,
Your sweet face seems,
To haunt my dreams,
My Lili of the lamplight,
My own Lili Marlene.

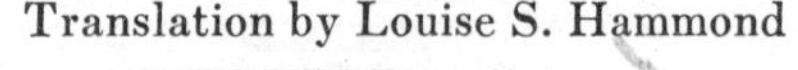

Translation by Louise S. Hammond

Music by Lio Hsüch-An

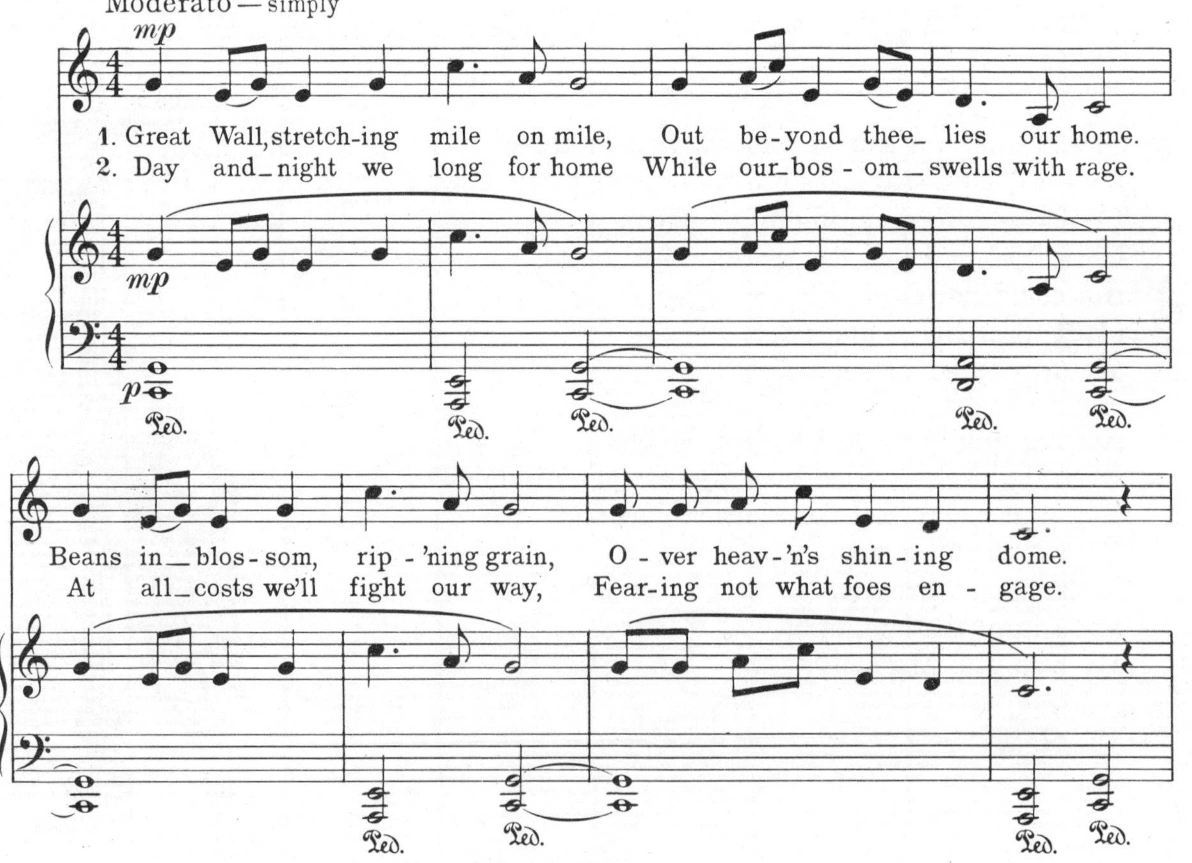
Moderato — simply
mp
1. Great Wall, stretch-ing mile on mile, Out be-yond thee_ lies our home.
2. Day and_night we long for home While our_bos - om_swells with rage.
mp
p
Beans in_blos-som, rip - 'ning grain, O - ver heav-'n's shin-ing dome.
At all_costs we'll fight our way, Fear-ing not what foes en - gage.

Song of the Great Wall

Since 1931 mass singing by the people of China has reached phenomenal heights. Patriotic songs have played an important role in uniting them in common resistance. The "Song of the Great Wall" is in Chinese folk-song style and shows less Western influence than many of the more recent songs.

Since the_ e - vil days have come Rape and_ mur - der_ fill the land;_
Great Wall, stretch-ing mile on mile, We_ will_ build an - oth - er wall_

Ped. * Ped. * Ped. * Ped. *

poco rit.

Chil - dren scat-tered, par - ents killed, More than hu-man hearts_ can stand!
Of the_ faith of band - ed men, All for one and one___ for all.

p

poco rit.

Ped. Ped. * Ped. Ped. *

MOSCOW

One of the stirring Red Army songs that have come to us from the Soviet Union.

English lyric by Olga Paul

Music by Dan and Din Pokrass

Allegro moderato

mf

1. In the dawn's light faint-ly gleam - ing, Stand the an-cient Krem - lin
2. Days are bright and grow-ing long - er, While the streets grow loud - er
3. When the day is slow-ly fad - ing, Twi-light falls and brings re -

mf

Left hand always staccato

walls, And the land no long-er dream-ing Now a-wakes as morn-ing
still, Chil-dren's voic - es ev - er strong-er Now are heard more loud and
lease From the hard-ships of pa - rad - ing Ev-'ning sud - den - ly brings

calls. Though the winds are cold - ly blow - ing, Streets be -
shrill. May-time flow - ers spread their splen - dor O - ver
peace. 'Tis the time for meet - ing lov - ers In the

mf

gin to hum with noise,___ And the sun with splen-dor glow - ing,__ Greets the
Mos-cow's an - cient streets,__ Men and wom - en hom-age ren - der,__ Ev - 'ry
gar - den, in the park,___ While the twi - light gent - ly hov - ers__ Till it's
land with all its joys.___
one with joy re - peats.___
night, and all is dark.___
f Chorus
We'll shout a - loud,_ For
we are proud,_ Our pow - er is in - vin - ci - ble!___ We'll
ne'er dis - band,_ We'll al - ways stand_ To - geth - er for dear Mos - cow's land.__
Ped.

God Save the King

Percy Scholes in his Oxford Companion to Music *says, "This must be the best known tune in the world. It is sung throughout the British Empire under the above title, throughout the United States of America as 'My Country, 'Tis of Thee', throughout the German Reich as 'Heil Dir in Siegerkranz', and in many other countries under other names." The tune, he claims, has no composer. It is apparently a recasting of folk song and plain song elements appearing as far back as the sixteenth and early seventeenth centuries. Its great popularity dates from 1745, the year of the second Jacobite rebellion, when it was sung in all the theatres of London and used as the rallying song of the House of Hanover.*

Allegro maestoso
mf
1. God save our gra - cious King, Long live our no - ble King,
2. O Lord and God a - rise, Scat - ter his en - e - mies,
3. Thy choic - est gifts in store On him be pleased to pour,
mf
Left hand with octaves ad lib.

God save the King! Send him vic - to - ri - ous, Hap - py and
And make them fall. Con - found their pol - i - tics, Frus-trate their
Long may he reign! May he de - fend our laws And ev - er
broader
glo - ri - ous, Long to reign o - ver us, God save the King!
knav - ish tricks, On Thee our hopes we fix, God save the King!
give us cause To sing with heart and voice, God save the King!
broader

NOTE: The song has never been the official British national anthem, though it has been sung generally with that significance. But on October 20, 1946, in St. Paul's Cathedral, King George lent his presence and approval to a change in the traditional form. In an effort to express the ideal of world brotherhood, symbolized in the United Nations, the second stanza printed above was discarded. The new version replaces that stanza with the old third, and adds a new third stanza, written almost a century ago but never generally accepted. The new third stanza is:

Nor on this land alone,
But be God's mercies known
From shore to shore.
Lord, make the nation see
That men should brothers be,
And form one family
The wide world o'er.

Rev. W. E. Hickson (1803-1870)

NO PASARAN

FREIHEIT

(SALUTE TO FREEDOM)

This is the song of the Thaelmann Battalion, the first unit of the International Brigades to arrive in Spain. It was largely the heroism of this Battalion that saved Madrid in 1936 when Franco was at the city's gates. Only a handful of the original 500 men in the battalion survived the Civil War.

Words by Karl Ernst **Music by Peter Daniel**

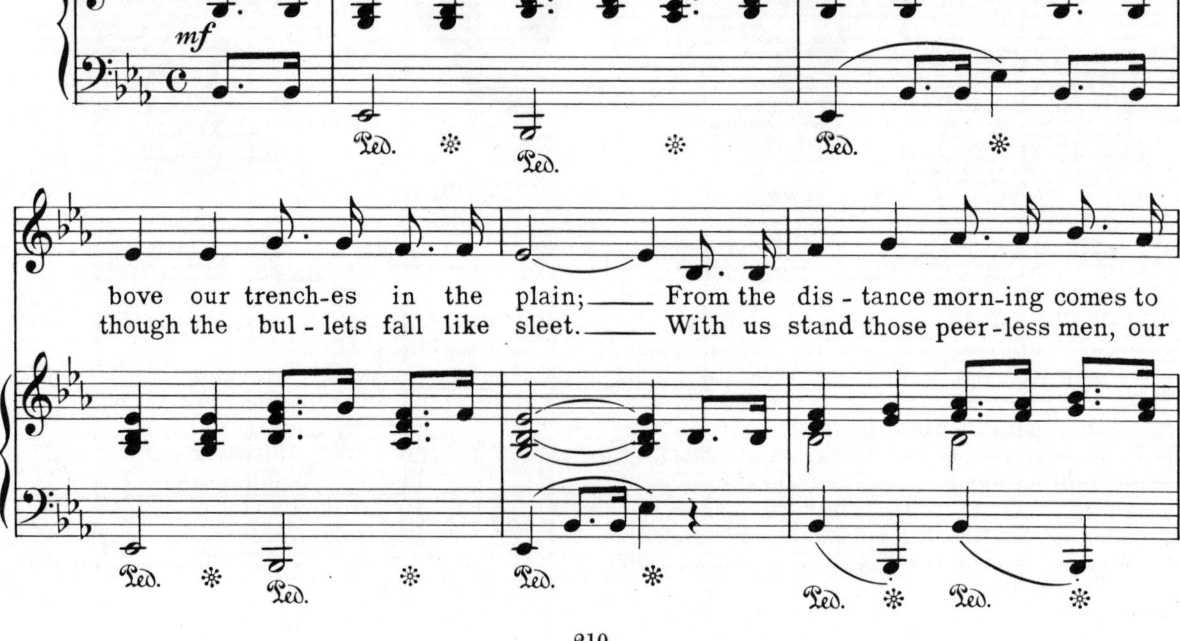
Resolutely
mf
1. Span - ish heav - ens spread their bril - liant star - light High a -
2. We'll not yield a foot to Fran - co's fac - ists, Ev - en
mf
bove our trench-es in the plain; From the dis - tance morn-ing comes to
though the bul - lets fall like sleet. With us stand those peer-less men, our

Chorus
greet us, Call-ing us to bat-tle once a-gain.
com-rades, And for us there can be no re-treat.
Far off is our
land, Yet read - y we stand, We're fight-ing and win-ning for
you, Free - dom!

3.

Beat the drums! Bayonets, charge!
Forward, march! Victory our reward!
With our scarlet banner! Smash their column!
Thaelmann Battalion! Ready, forward, march!
Chorus:

The Peat-Bog Soldiers

It is generally believed that this song originated and was first sung in the Börgermoor concentration camp in 1933. Pierre Martinot, designer of this book, who was a prisoner in Dachau in 1944-45, says that the old prisoners there claimed that the song was created and first sung in Dachau, and that it was carried from there by underground to Börgermoor.

With determination
mp
1. Far and wide as the eye can wan-der, Heath and bog are ev-'ry-where.
2. Up and down the guards are pac-ing, No one, no one can go through;
3. But for us there is no com-plain-ing, Win-ter will in time be past.
mp

Not a bird sings out to cheer us, Oaks are stand - ing gaunt and bare.
Flight would mean a sure death fac - ing, Guns and barbed wire greet our view.
One day we shall cry, re - joic - ing: Home-land, dear, you're mine at last.
mf Chorus
1.&2. We are the peat-bog sol-diers, We're march-ing with our spades to the bog.
3. Then will the peat-bog sol - diers March no more with their spades to the bog.
mf

TACHANKA

A tachanka is a four-wheeled farm wagon much used in the Ukraine. During the Civil Wars the partisans set up in it any kind of gun they could get hold of and thus improvised a sort of mobile fire-power which for the first time offset the traditional and historical cavalry superiority of the Cossacks and the regular Tsarist army. So it has a sentimental and class significance to the Soviets.

Adapted from the English lyric by Olga Paul

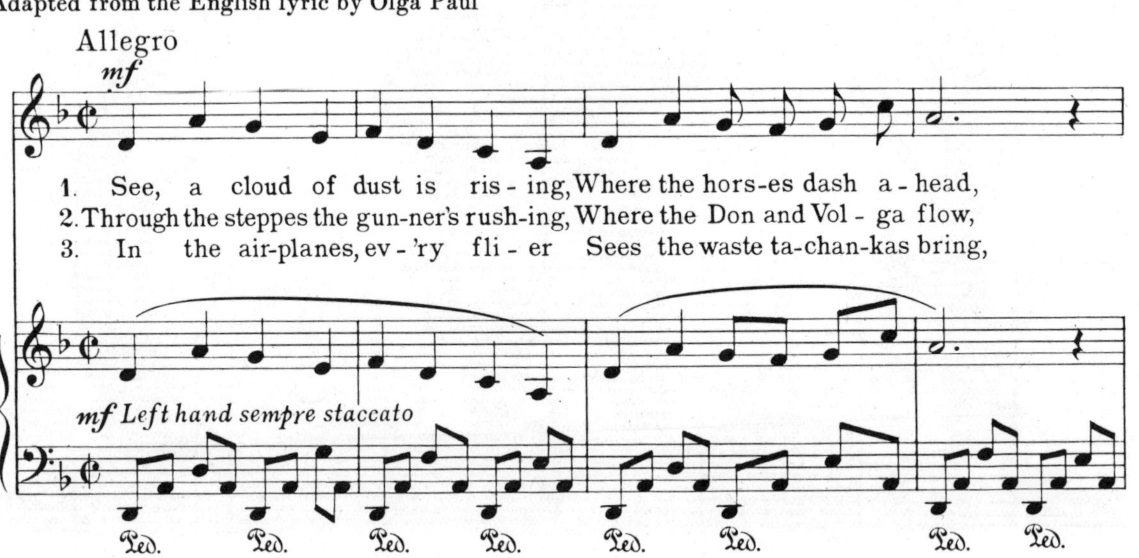
Allegro
mf
1. See, a cloud of dust is ris - ing, Where the hors-es dash a - head,
2. Through the steppes the gun-ner's rush-ing, Where the Don and Vol - ga flow,
3. In the air-planes, ev - 'ry fli - er Sees the waste ta-chan-kas bring,
mf Left hand sempre staccato
Ped. Ped. Ped. Ped. Ped. Ped. Ped. Ped.

And their dan-ger rec-og-niz - ing, Bird has flown and beast has fled.
With the ta-chan-ka he'll be crush - ing Ev - 'ry en - e - my and foe.
Then while soar-ing ev- er high - er, With de - light will gai - ly sing.
Chorus
Ah, ta - chan - ka, lit-tle Ros-tov wa - gon, Of your beau-ty we are proud,
mf
Lit - tle wag-on of the land of A - zor, Dash - ing wild-ly through the crowd.
mf

WALTZING MATILDA
A nineteenth-century Australian bush song.
Allegro
mf
1. Once a jol - ly swag - man sat be-side the bil - la-bong, Un - der the
2. Down came a jum - buck to drink be-side the bil - la-bong, Up jumped the
shade of a cou - li - bah tree, And he sang as he sat and
swag - man and seized him with glee. And he sang as he talked to that
wait - ed by the bil - la-bong,
jum-buck in his tuck-er-bag,
"You'll come a - waltz - ing Ma - til - da, with me."
poco rit.
Waltz tempo
Waltz-ing Ma-til - da, waltz-ing Ma - til - da, You'll come a - waltz-ing Ma-til-da, with

me. {And he sang as he sat and— wait-ed by the bil-la-bong, / And he sang as he talked to that jum-buck in his tuck-er-bag,} "You'll come a-

waltz-ing, Ma-til-da, with me."

3. Down came the stockman, riding on his thoroughbred,
Down came the troopers, one, two, three.
"Where's the jolly jumbuck you've got in your tuckerbag?
You'll come a-waltzing, Matilda, with me."

CHORUS

Waltzing Matilda, waltzing Matilda,
"You'll come a-waltzing, Matilda, with me."
"Where's the jolly jumbuck you've got in your tuckerbag?
You'll come a-waltzing, Matilda, with me."

4. Up jumped the swagman and plunged into the billabong,
"You'll never catch me alive," cried he,
And his ghost may be heard as you ride beside the billabong,
"You'll come a-waltzing, Matilda, with me."

CHORUS

Waltzing Matilda, waltzing Matilda,
"You'll come a-waltzing, Matilda, with me."
And his ghost may be heard as you ride beside the billabong,
"You'll come a-waltzing, Matilda, with me."

Note: swagman—a hobo; billabong—a water hole in a dried-up river bed; waltzing Matilda—the bundle on a stick carried by a hobo; jumbuck—a small lamb; tuckerbag—knapsack.

LOS NACIONALES

LOS CUATRO GENERALES

(THE FOUR GENERALS)

"The four generals were Franco, Mola, Varela, and Queipo de Llano. Each was in command of one of the four columns advancing on Madrid. The name 'fifth column' was first given by the Spanish fascists to their own undercover agents behind the Loyalist lines who were cooperating with the enemy columns." (Program notes from Six Songs for Democracy, *Music Products, Inc., publishers.)*

Translation by Anne Bromberger and Leonard Mins

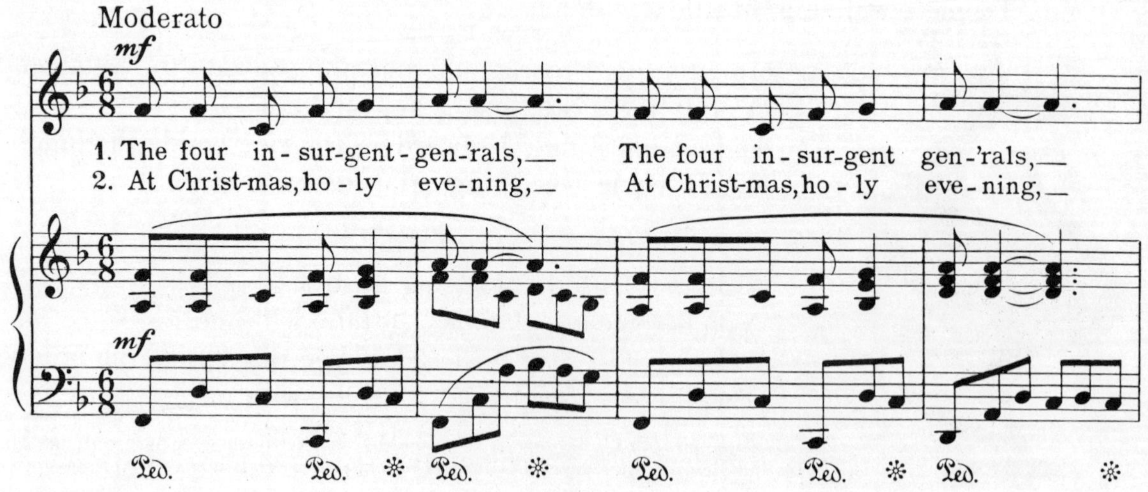
Moderato
mf
1. The four in-sur-gent-gen-'rals,— The four in-sur-gent gen-'rals,—
2. At Christ-mas, ho-ly eve-ning,— At Christ-mas, ho-ly eve-ning,—
mf

The four in - sur-gent gen-'rals, Ma - mi - ta Mi - a,* They tried to be -
At Christ-mas, ho - ly eve-ning, Ma - mi - ta Mi - a, They'll all ___ be

broader

Verses 1–5 | Verse 6

tray us, They tried to be - tray us. ___ sun-der. ___
hang-ing, They'll all ___ be hang-ing. ___

broader *a tempo*

3. Madrid, you wondrous city, *(3 times)*
Mamita Mia,
They wanted to take you, *(2 times)*

4. But your courageous children, *(3 times)*
Mamita Mia,
They did not disgrace you, *(2 times)*

5. And all your tears of sorrow, *(3 times)*
Mamita Mia,
We shall avenge them, *(2 times)*

6. And all our age-old bondage, *(3 times)*
Mamita Mia,
We'll break asunder, *(2 times)*

*My Little Mother

BATTLE HYMN OF THE REPUBLIC

In 1861, Julia Ward Howe, on a visit to some army camps, heard the soldiers singing a grim chant, "John Brown's Body," to the tune of a camp-meeting hymn, "Say, Brothers, Will You Meet Us?" Deeply moved by the scene, she later wrote for the fine, sturdy tune the words of the "Battle Hymn," one of the most stirring poems to come out of the Civil War. It became the marching song of the Northern armies, and is undoubtedly one of the best of all marching songs. "John Brown's Body," however, still remains popular.

Words by Julia Ward Howe

Maestoso

mf

1. Mine__ eyes have seen the glo - ry of the
2. I have seen Him in the watch - fires of a
3. I have read a fier - y gos - pel writ in

Ped. Ped. * Ped. *

com - ing of the Lord; He is tramp-ling out the vin - tage where the
hun - dred circ - ling camps; They have build - ed Him an al - tar in the
burn - ish'd rows of steel: "As ye deal with My con - tem - ners, so with

Ped. * Ped. * Ped. * Ped. *

grapes of wrath are stored; He hath loos'd the fate - ful light - ning of His
ev - 'ning dews and damps: I can read His right - eous sen - tence by the
you My grace shall deal"; Let the He - ro, born of wom - an, crush the
Ped. ※ Ped. ※ Ped. ※ Ped. ※

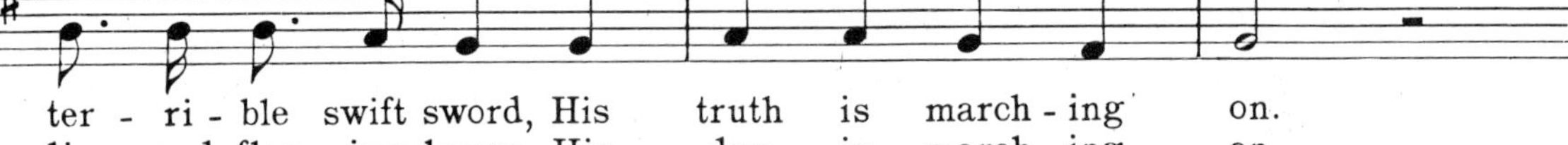
ter - ri - ble swift sword, His truth is march - ing on.
dim and flar - ing lamps, His day is march - ing on.
ser - pent with His heel, Since God is march - ing on.

Ped. Ped. Ped. Ped. Ped. Ped. Ped. Ped. Ped. Ped. ※

Chorus
Glo - ry, glo - ry Hal - le - lu - jah! Glo - ry, glo - ry Hal - le - lu - jah!

Ped. ※ Ped. Ped. ※

Glo - ry, glo - ry Hal - le - lu - jah! His truth is march-ing on.

John Brown's Body

1. John Brown's body lies a mould'ring in the ground,
John Brown's body lies a mould'ring in the ground,
John Brown's body lies a mould'ring in the ground,
But his soul goes marching on.
Chorus:

2. He's gone to be a soldier in the army of the Lord,
He's gone to be a soldier in the army of the Lord,
He's gone to be a soldier in the army of the Lord,
His soul is marching on.
Chorus:

3. John Brown died that the slave might be free,
John Brown died that the slave might be free,
John Brown died that the slave might be free,
But his soul goes marching on.
Chorus:

4. The stars of heaven are looking kindly down,
The stars of heaven are looking kindly down,
The stars of heaven are looking kindly down,
On the grave of old John Brown.
Chorus:

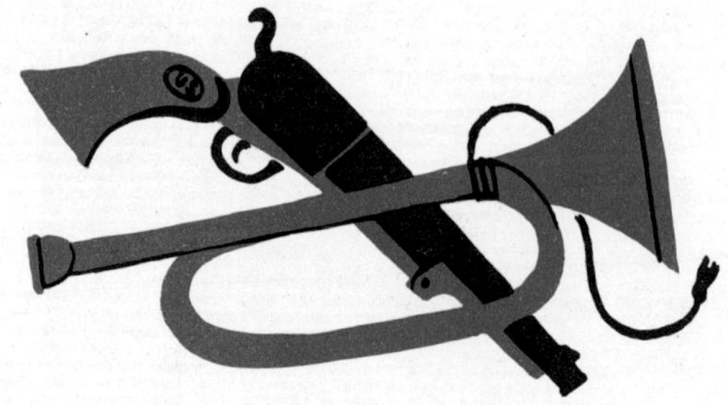

CHORUS

Glory, glory, Hallelujah!
Glory, glory, Hallelujah!
Glory, glory, Hallelujah!
His soul goes marching on.

La Marseillaise

Written by Rouget de Lisle, a young officer in the French army stationed in Strasbourg in 1792. It was played at a patriotic banquet at Marseilles, and printed copies were given to the revolutionary forces then marching on Paris. They entered Paris singing this song, and to it they marched to the Tuileries on August 10. Ironically, Rouget de Lisle was himself a royalist and refused to take the oath of allegiance to the new constitution. He was imprisoned and barely escaped the guillotine.

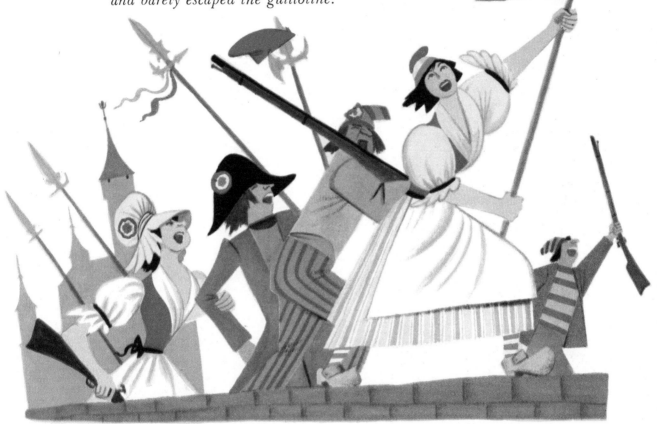

Words and Music by Rouget de Lisle

Allegro
f
1. Ye sons of France, a-wake to glo - ry! Hark! Hark! the peo-ple bid you
All-ons, en-fants de la pat - ri - e, Le jour de gloire est arr - i -
f
col 8
Ped. Ped. Ped. Ped. Ped.

rise! Your chil-dren, wives, and grand-sires hoar-y Be-hold their
vé. Con-tre nous de la tyr-ann-i-e L'è-ten-dard
col 8
tears and hear their cries! Be-hold their tears and hear their
sang-lant est le-vé. L'è-ten-dard sang-lant est le-
col 8
cries! Shall hate-ful ty-rants, mis-chief breed-ing, With hire-ling
vé. En-ten-dez vous dans les cam-pagn-es Mu-girces
hosts a ruf-fi-an band, Af-fright and des-o-late the
fér-o-ces sol-dats? Ils vien-nent jus-que dans nos

f Chorus
land While peace and lib-er-ty lie bleed-ing? To arms, to arms, ye
bras E-gorg-er vos fils, vos com-pagn-es: Aux ar-mes, Ci-toy-
brave! Th'a-veng-ing sword un-sheathe! March on! March
ens! For-mez vos ba-taill-ons! Mar-chons, mar-
on! all hearts re-solved On lib-er-ty or death.
chons, Qu'un sank im-pur A-breuve nos sill-ons!
col 8s ad lib.
EGALITE FRATERNITE LIBERTE

The Minstrel Boy

The melody is an old Irish air, "The Moreen." The song was very popular in America in the early days of the nineteenth century.

Moderato
mf
1. The min - strel boy_ to the war is gone, In the ranks of death _ you'll
2. The min - strel fell,_ but the foe-man's chain Could not bring that proud soul_
find him; His fa - ther's sword_ he has gird - ed on, And his wild harp slung be -
un - der; The harp he lov'd_ ne-'er spoke a - gain, For he tore its chords a -
3-5
2 4 5
mf
Ped. Ped. Ped. *
Ped. Ped. Ped. *

hind him. "Land of song!" said the war-rior bard, "Though all the world be -
sun - der; And said, "No chain shall_ sul - ly thee, Thou soul of love and
trays_ thee, One sword, at least,_ thy_ rights shall guard, One_
brav - er - y Thy songs were made_ for the pure and free, They shall
faith-ful harp_ shall_praise thee!"
nev - er sound in_ slav - 'ry."

Come, Fellow Workers

This song, according to Zilphia Horton of the Highlander Folk School, Monteagle, Tennessee, is one which she learned about six years ago from Miss Cora Deng, who at that time was head of the Industrial Division of the YWCA in China. She in turn learned it from the Chinese industrial workers.

Allegro

mf

1. Come, fel-low work-ers, hung ho hai ho, Seek e-man-ci-pa-tion,
2. Come, fel-low work-ers, hung ho hai ho, Fight_ for — Free-dom,

mf

hung ho hai ho, Ho! Ho! ho tsi-li

f

hung ho, Ho! Ho! hung-yo-lo-yo, Hai!_______

CHRISTMAS CAROLS

Christmas Carols

THE JOYOUS music of the carol is a pagan note in our church services. In the middle ages carols were secular songs—often dance tunes, as "carole" indicates. In England and Europe, the carol was danced usually by a chain of male and female dancers, moving with clasped hands while the stanza was sung, then marking time while they sang the burden. The carol was so much cherished by the people that the church sagely accepted it, pagan connotations and all.

Even today in the Cathedral of Seville the dance origin of the old sacred music is preserved on certain feast days when the choir boys move to the stately music with castanets, dancing an ancient dance. And in Central and South American communities where the Spanish missionaries traveled, the custom also survives. The Puerto Ricans celebrate Christmas with many dance songs, and in the southwest United States the Pueblo Indians, in full dance costume, enter church on Christmas Eve to greet the Christ child, beating on drums in dance rhythm.

The dramatic origins of the old folk carols were not ignored by the church either. The theatrical quality of the music was given scope in church mystery plays, in Boar's Head and May Day processions, in the entirely pagan ceremony of the Yule log. One of the first countries to incorporate in the church the drama so beloved by the people was Italy. There, in the thirteenth century, St. Francis in an attempt to humanize religion established the Praesepium, or Creche, still used in Catholic churches at Christmas time. An infant's cradle was set up in St.

Francis' church and the parish children brought gifts, like the Magi. Special songs grew up about this ceremony, and little dramas, enacted by the young people. Many lovely lullaby carols date from that early Italian custom. And perhaps as a result of this Mediterranean celebration of Christmas, other churches in Europe began to accept some part of the traditional mystery plays as their Christmas ceremony. In Germany the beautiful carol "Joseph Lieber" dates from such a dramatization of the nativity, as its dialogue form still proclaims. The English Coventry Carol is another fragment of a mystery play which has become part of church ceremony. The famous "Adeste Fideles" has its origins buried in obscurity, but many scholars now believe that it too was part of a Christmas drama, music for a dance performed about the altar and the Praesepium.

As for the unchristian traditions of the old carols, dating back to Druid worship or Roman Saturnalia, they were adopted wholesale, although in those days their symbolism was more readily apparent than it is now. For instance, the holly and the ivy so often referred to in English and German Christmas carols springs from Saturnalia festivals. The Romans always decorated their homes, at the time of these feasts, with holly and other evergreens. Later, early Christians in England invested holly with a mystic significance and hung it in windows to ward off pagan foes. In much of Europe, the use of holly was banned because of its Roman origins. In England, as so many of the carols testify, the use of holly became so much a part of the national folk tradition that the church accepted the symbol in spite of its pre-Christian origins. Scholars, delving into the holly and ivy symbolism, incidentally, bring out many fascinating details about it, some illustrated by the old carols. In early English folk custom the two plants had a sexual significance—the holly as the male, the ivy as the female. In houses in some shires of England the ivy was used as a fertility symbol. In East Kent as late as the eighteenth century, the villagers burned effigies which were known as the Holly Boy and the Ivy Girl in order to bring about a better harvest. And the carols reveal that there were games played around Christmas time to establish male or female supremacy in the house for the rest of the year. Some of the old songs speak of excluding Ivy and her women from the hall. And so far was this battle carried between holly and ivy that according to another English folk custom the women of the community were allowed to accept no gifts at all on Christmas day!

The mistletoe has no Christian origin. The ancient Druids used the green plant in their religious ceremonies, and in England and France where the Druid sects were predominant the plant became a part of national tradition and later of the Christmas ceremony without regard to its significance.

As for the Wassail which often appears in Christmas carols, that once used to be an old Anglo-Saxon drinking toast, "Waes Hael," which means "Be in health." The Saxons drank this toast to the Lord at their traditional feasts, and the old carols so frequently celebrated the custom that it too became part of Christmas.

The Boar's Head which is also often mentioned in carols has no particular Christian significance either. The story goes that a young Oxford student was walking through the hills near his college one day when a wild boar rushed out at him. The boy thrust the copy of Aristotle which he was studying down the boar's throat and thus escaped the animal's jaws. Later his fellow students served the head of the boar in thanksgiving for his amazing escape. Out of this, according to legend, a custom grew up which was for some unknown reason associated with Christmas. Throughout the land the boar's head was traditionally borne into the Christmas feasts by the cooks, wreathed in bay leaves and rosemary as the songs tell us. The ceremony still exists at Oxford.

Perhaps it was these frivolous beginnings of the Christmas carols that made them so hated by the Puritans, who during their Reformation banned all such songs. Even Christmas day itself and its festivities were officially abolished during the seventeenth century as "The Old Heathen's Feasting Day in honour to Saturn their Idol-God, the Papist's Massing Day, the Profane Man's Ranting Day, the Superstitious Man's Idol Day, the Multitude's Idle Day, Satan's—that Adversary's—Working Day, the True Christian Man's Fasting Day. . . . We are persuaded no one thing more hindereth the Gospel work all the year long, than doth the observation of that Idol Day once in a year, having so many days of cursed observation with it."

But although for two centuries or more after this wave of reformation no new carols were written, the old ones were preserved in the affections of the people, and we still have many of them today. And if there was a gap of two or three hundred years before new songs were added to carol literature, that gap has been more than made up for since. In the middle of the last century, some scholars began to publish collections of the old songs, carol singing came into vogue again, and new authors added their contributions. As the vogue spread, carols from every part of Europe were added to the English collections, and our carol literature in English-speaking churches today is a truly international one, as this section indicates. Only scholars trace the ancient and unchristian origins of the songs now. For the average man the songs, old or new, are as truly a part of Christianity's great feast day as the church services. Their lovely, gay quality had added more than anything else to the joyous nature of Christ's birthday.

Angels We Have Heard on High

Telesphorus, Bishop of Rome, A.D. 129, ordained that "In the Holy Night of the Nativity of our Lord and Saviour, all shall solemnly sing the 'Angel's Hymn.'" And so the "Angel's Hymn," which today exists in many versions, became the first Christmas hymn of the church.

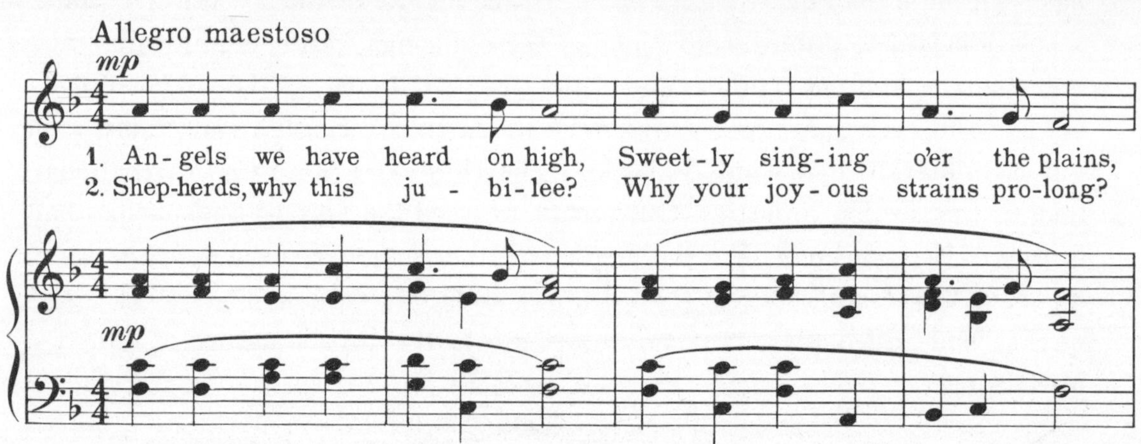
Allegro maestoso
mp
1. An-gels we have heard on high, Sweet-ly sing-ing o'er the plains,
2. Shep-herds, why this ju - bi-lee? Why your joy-ous strains pro-long?
mp

p
And the moun-tains in re-ply, Ech-o-ing their joy-ous strains.
What the glad-some tid-ings be Which in-spire your heav'n-ly song?
Glo - - - - - - ri-a in ex-cel-sis De-o,
mf
Glo - - - - - - ri-a in ex-cel-sis De - o.
f

3. Come to Bethlehem and see
Him Whose birth the angels sing;
Come, adore on bended knee,
Christ the Lord, the new-born King.
Gloria, etc.

4. See Him in a manger laid,
Whom the choirs of angels praise;
Mary, Joseph, lend your aid,
While our hearts in love we raise.
Gloria, etc.

O Little Town of Bethlehem

The verses were written by Phillips Brooks, Bishop of Massachusetts, and sent out as a Sunday school song. It has since become one of the most popular of the American Christmas carols.

Words by Phillips Brooks **Music by Lewis H. Redner**

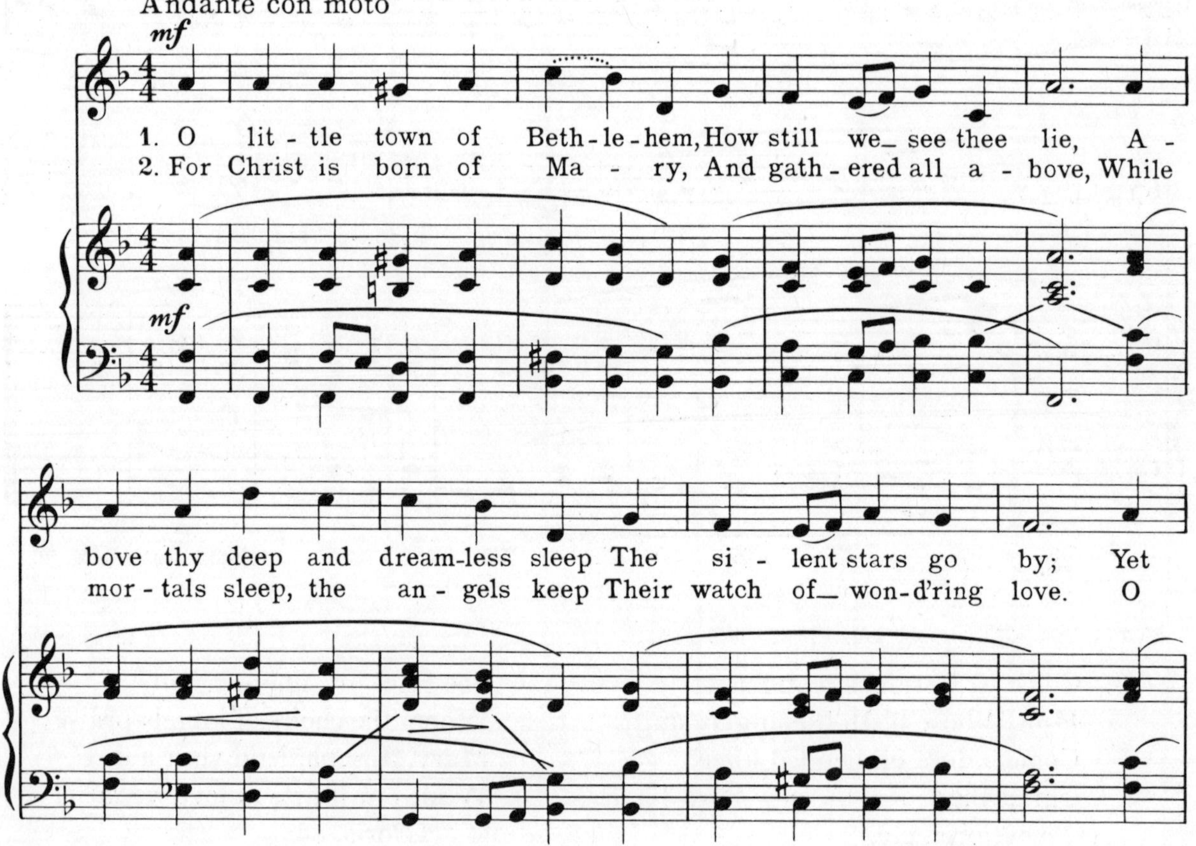

Andante con moto
mf
1. O lit - tle town of Beth - le - hem, How still we_ see thee lie, A - bove thy deep and dream-less sleep The si - lent stars go by; Yet
2. For Christ is born of Ma - ry, And gath - ered all a - bove, While mor - tals sleep, the an - gels keep Their watch of_ won-d'ring love. O
mf

mf
in thy dark streets shin - eth The ev - er - last - ing light, The
morn - ing stars, to - geth - er Pro - claim the ho - ly birth, And
mf
hopes and fears of all the years, Are met in thee to - night.
prais - es sing to God the King, And peace to men on earth.

3.

How silently, how silently,
The wondrous gift is given;
So God imparts to human hearts
The blessing of His heaven.
No ear may hear His coming,
But in this world of sin,
Where meek souls will receive Him still,
The dear Christ enters in.

4.

O holy Child of Bethlehem,
Descend to us, we pray,
Cast out our sins, and enter in,
Be born in us today.
We hear the Christmas angels
The great glad tidings tell:
O come to us, abide with us,
Our Lord Emmanuel.

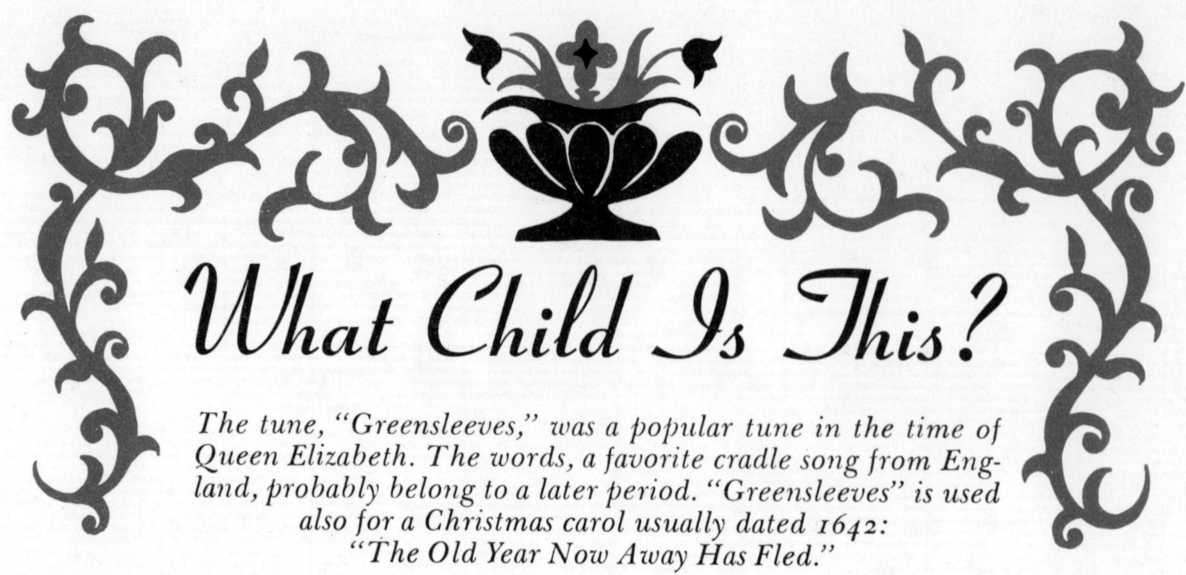

What Child Is This?

The tune, "Greensleeves," was a popular tune in the time of Queen Elizabeth. The words, a favorite cradle song from England, probably belong to a later period. "Greensleeves" is used also for a Christmas carol usually dated 1642: "The Old Year Now Away Has Fled."

Words by H. C. Dix

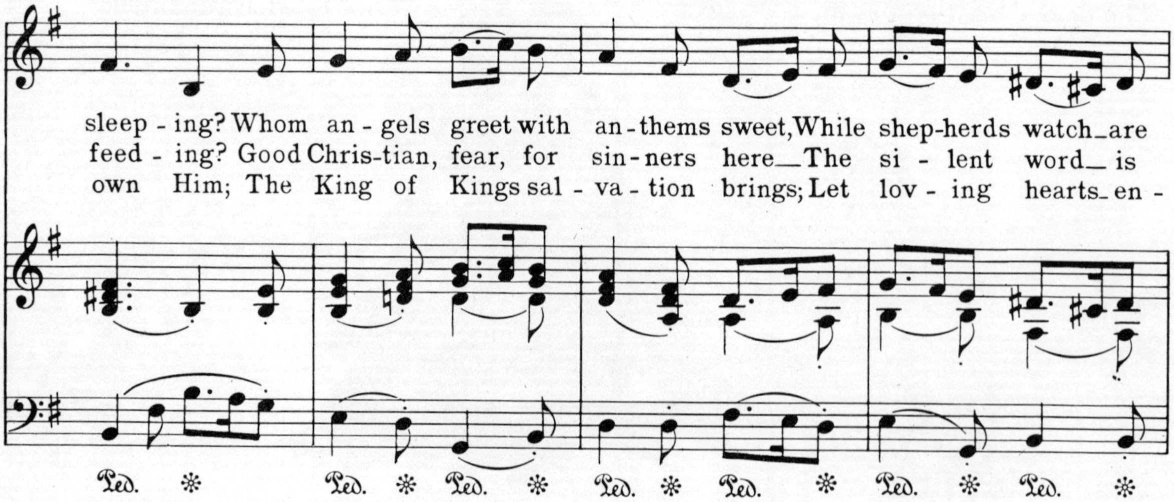

Allegretto

mf

1. What child is this,— who, laid to rest,— On Ma - ry's lap— is
2. Why lies He in— such mean es - tate,—Where ox and ass— are
3. So bring Him in - cense, gold, and myrrh, Come peas - ant, king,— to

sleep - ing? Whom an - gels greet with an - thems sweet, While shep - herds watch— are
feed - ing? Good Chris - tian, fear, for sin - ners here— The si - lent word— is
own Him; The King of Kings sal - va - tion brings; Let lov - ing hearts— en -

f

keep - ing? This, this_ is Christ the King;_Whom shep-herds guard and
plead - ing; Nails, spear,shall pierce Him through, The Cross be borne for
throne Him. Raise, raise the song on high,_The Vir - gin sing_her

an - gels sing: Haste, haste to bring Him laud, The Babe, the Son_of Ma - ry.
me, for you: Hail, hail, the Word made flesh, The Babe, the Son_of Ma - ry.
lul - la - by: Joy, joy,_for Christ is born, The Babe, the Son_of Ma - ry.

Good Christian Men, Rejoice

A German carol of the fourteenth century, originally written half in Latin and half in German. In 1540 John Weddeburn translated the German half into English: "In dulci jubilo, Now let us sing with mirth and joy." The melody, slightly changed, is now sung to the words "Good Christian Men, Rejoice."

Translation by Rev. Dr. John Mason Neale

Allegro
mf
1. Good Chris-tian men, re - joice___ With heart and soul and voice;___
2. Good Chris-tian men, re - joice___ With heart and soul and voice,___
3. Good Chris-tian men, re - joice___ With heart and soul and voice,___
mf

Give ye heed to what we say; News! News! Jesus Christ is
Now ye hear of end-less bliss: Joy! Joy! Je-sus Christ was
Now ye need not fear the grave: Peace! Peace! Je-sus Christ was
mf
born to-day! Ox and ass be-fore Him bow, And He is in the
born for this. He hath ope'd the heav'n-ly door, And man is bless-ed
born to save. Calls you one and calls you all, To gain His ev-er-
mp
man-ger now; Christ is born to-day! Christ is born to-day!
ev-er-more; Christ was born for this! Christ was born for this!
last-ing hall: Christ was born to save! Christ was born to save!

Jeannette, Isabella

In Provence and southern Europe the torches, or candles, of the ancient Jewish Hanukkah, the Festival of Lights, played an important part in the Christmas celebrations. This carol, from Provence, is a beautiful example of the torch songs of that period.

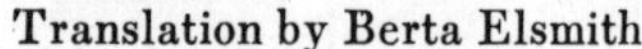

Translation by Berta Elsmith

Lightly

mf

1. Torch-es here,_ Jean-nette, Is-a-bel-la! Torch-es here to His cra-dle run! This is Je-sus, good folk of the vil-lage, Christ_ is
2. Wrong it is, when the Ba-by is sleep-ing, Wrong it is___ to shout_ so loud. Now you there, and you oth-ers, be qui-et! For at_ a

born, 'tis Ma - ry call - ing. Ah! Ah! Ah! What a love - ly
sound our Je - sus wak - ens. Hush! Hush! Hush! He is sleep - ing
Moth - er! Ah! Ah! Ah! What a love - ly Child!
sound - ly, Hush! Hush! Hush! Do but see Him sleep!

3.

Who comes there in this way knocking, knocking?
Who comes there knocking, knocking like that?
Open then! We have put on a plate
Some very good cakes, which here we carry,
Toc! toc! toc! open wide the door then,
Toc! toc! toc! let us have a feast!

4.

Softly now in the narrow stable,
Softly now for a moment stay.
Come quite near! How charming is Jesus!
Oh look, how white! Oh see, how rosy!
Do! do! do! let the Baby slumber!
Do! do! do! see the Baby smile!

Adeste Fideles

(O COME, ALL YE FAITHFUL)

"Adeste Fideles" is sung in Protestant and Catholic churches throughout the world. The tune, attributed to St. Bonaventura, is thought to be an old Latin carol, written originally to be danced and sung around the altar and the Praesepium in a Christmas drama.

Old Latin by J. Reading, 1692
English translation by Rev. F. Oakeley, 1841

Majestically

mf

1. Ad - es - te fi - de - les, lae - ti tri - um - phan - tes; Ve - ni - te, ve - ni - te in Beth - le - hem: Na - tum vi - de - te,

1. O come, all ye faith - ful, joy - ful and tri - umph - ant; O come ye, O come_ye to Beth - le - hem. Come and be - hold Him,

p
mf
Re - gem an - ge - lo - rum: Ve - ni - te ad - o - re - mus, Ve - ni - te ad - o -
born the King of an - gels: O come, let us a - dore Him, O come, let us a -
p
mf
f
re - mus, Ve - ni - te ad - o - re - mus Do - mi - num.
dore Him, O come, let us a - dore Him, Christ the Lord.
f

2. Sing, choirs of angels, sing in exultation,
Sing, all ye citizens of heav'n above:
Glory to God, in the highest:
O come, etc.

3. Yea Lord, we greet Thee, born this happy morning,
Jesus, to Thee be glory giv'n;
Word of the Father, now in flesh appearing:
O come, etc.

Good King Wenceslas

The tune is originally that of an old spring carol, "Tempus adest floridium." In 1853 Neale substituted for the words of the carol his legend of Good King Wenzel, King of Bohemia from A.D. 928 to 935, who was celebrated for his many kind acts to the poor.

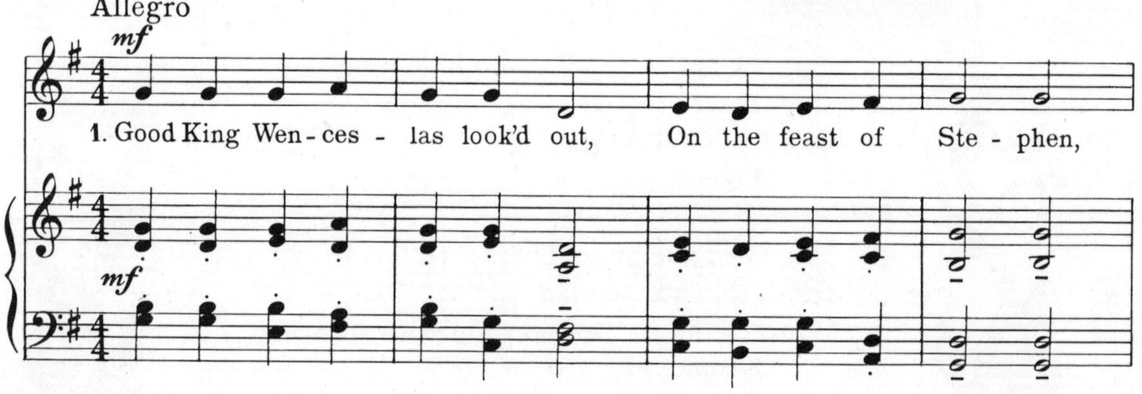
Allegro
mf
1. Good King Wen - ces - las look'd out, On the feast of Ste - phen,
mf

mp
When the snow lay round-a-bout, Deep and crisp and e - ven. Bright-ly shone the

moon that night, Though the frost was cru - el, When a poor man came in sight,

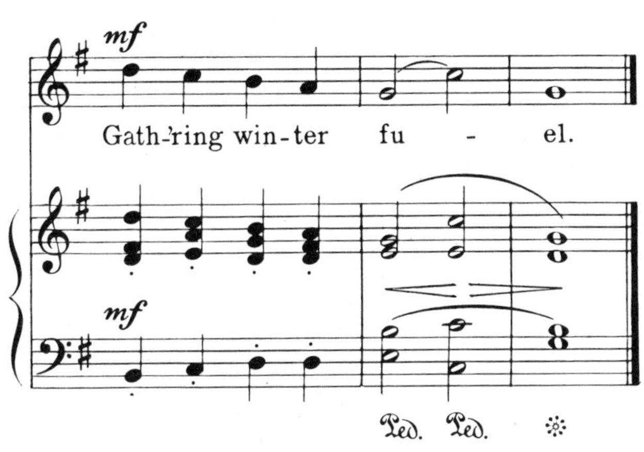
mf
Gath-'ring win-ter fu - el.
mf

2.

"Hither, page, and stand by me,
If thou knows't it telling,
Yonder peasant, who is he?
Where and what his dwelling?"
"Sire, he lives a good league hence,
Underneath the mountain,
Right against the forest fence,
By Saint Agnes' fountain."

3.

"Bring me flesh, and bring me wine,
Bring me pine-logs hither:
Thou and I shall see him dine,
When we bear them thither."
Page and monarch, forth they went,
Forth they went together;
Through the rude wind's wild lament
And the bitter weather.

4.

"Sire, the night is darker now,
And the wind grows stronger;
Fails my heart, I know not how;
I can go no longer."
"Mark my footsteps, my good page,
Tread thou in them boldly;
Thou shalt find the winter's rage
Freeze thy blood less coldly."

5.

In his master's steps he trod,
Where the snow lay dinted;
Heat was in the very sod
Which the Saint had printed.
Therefore, Christian men, be sure,
Wealth or rank possessing,
Ye who now will bless the poor,
Shall yourselves find blessing.

The Twelve Days of Christmas

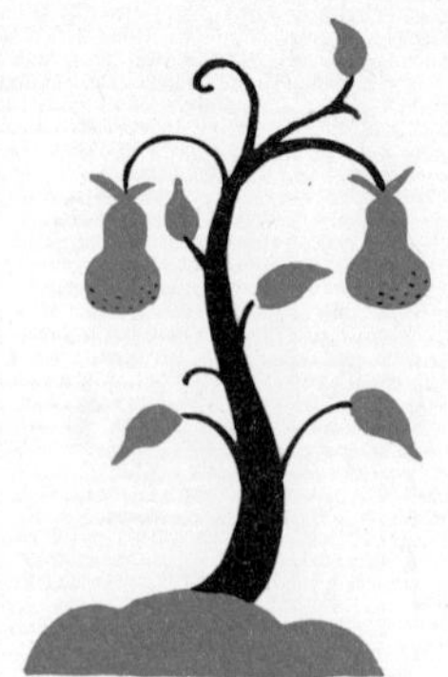

A very old and unusual cumulative carol from England. The twelve days of Christmas are those between Christmas day and Epiphany.

Gaily

mf

1. On the first day of Christ-mas My true love sent to me, A par - tridge in a pear tree.___ 2. On the se-cond day of Christ-mas my true love sent to me, two tur-tle doves and a par-tridge in a pear - tree. 3. On the

mf

Ped. Ped. Ped. Ped. * Ped. Ped. Ped. Ped. *

third day of Christ-mas, my true love sent to me. three French hens,
two tur-tle doves, and a par - tridge in a pear tree. 4. On the
fourth day of Christ-mas, my true love sent to me: four call-ing birds
three French hens

two tur-tle doves, and a par-tridge in a pear tree. 5. On the
fifth day of Christ-mas, my true love sent to me, five gold rings,
four calling birds. three French hens, two tur-tle doves, and a
Repeat for seventh day to twelfth day
par-tridge in a pear tree. 6. On the sixth day of Christ-mas, my
7. On the seventh day—etc.

6
5
true love sent to me, six geese a - lay - ing, (to 5) five gold_
seven swans a - swim-ming, (to 6)
eight maids a milk - ing, (to 7)
nine la - dies danc - ing, (to 8)
ten lords a - leap - ing, (to 9)
eleven pi - pers pi - ping, (to 10)
twelve drum-mers drum-ming, (to 11)
rings, four_call-ing birds, three French hens, two_tur-tle doves, and a
Ped. * Ped. * Ped. *
D.S.
par - tridge in a pear tree.___
D.S.

COVENTRY CAROL

This carol is said to have originated in a fifteenth-century Coventry play, The Pageant of the Shearmen and the Tailors. *The tune first appeared around 1591.*

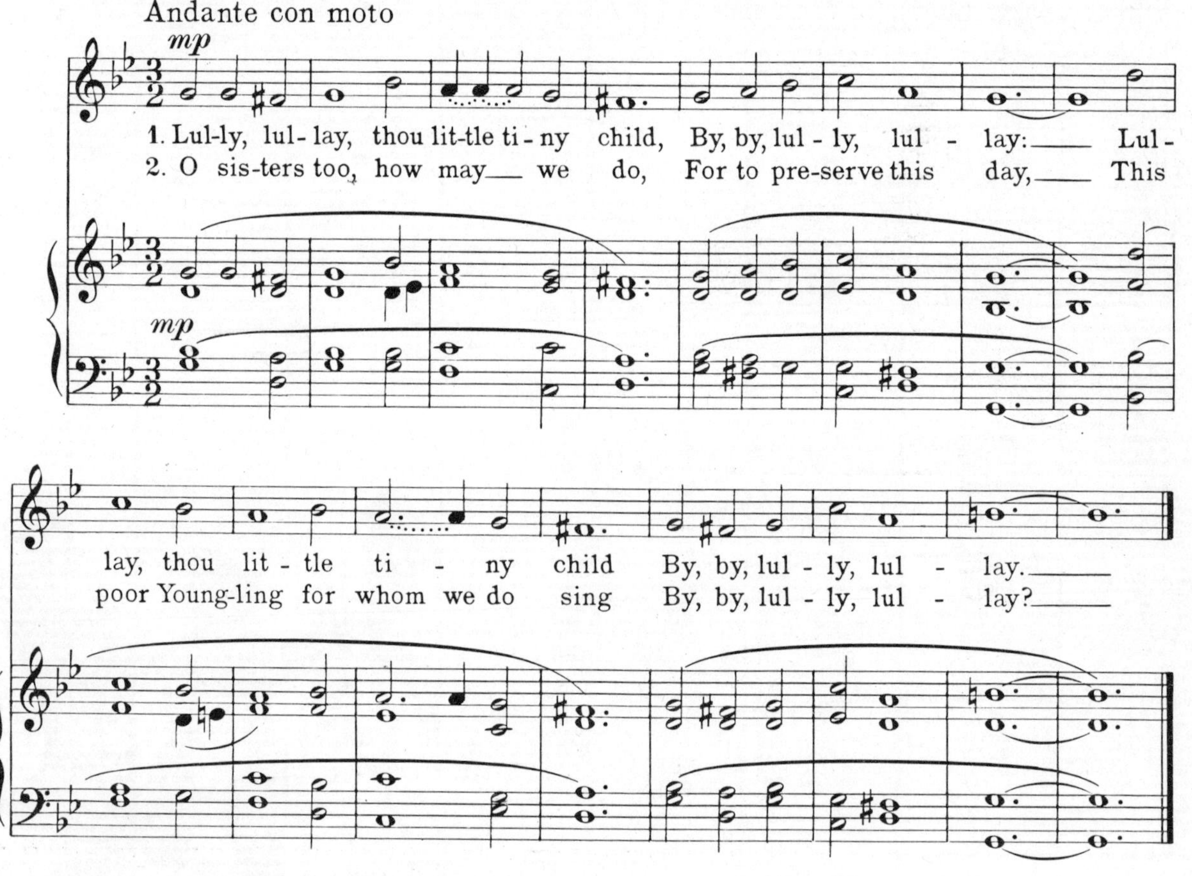

Andante con moto
mp
1. Lul-ly, lul-lay, thou lit-tle ti-ny child, By, by, lul-ly, lul-lay: Lul-lay, thou lit-tle ti-ny child By, by, lul-ly, lul-lay.
2. O sis-ters too, how may we do, For to pre-serve this day, This poor Young-ling for whom we do sing By, by, lul-ly, lul-lay?
mp

3.

Herod the king in his raging,
Chargéd he hath this day
His men of might, in his own sight
All children young to slay.

4.

Then woe is me, poor child for thee,
And ever mourn and say,
For thy parting nor say nor sing,
By, by, lully, lullay.

O SANCTISSIMA

(O THOU JOYFUL DAY)

A Latin hymn of the sixteenth century. The tune is a folk song of the Sicilian seas.

Andante con moto

mf

O sanc - tis - si - ma, O pi - is - si - ma, Dul - cis
1. & 2. O thou joy - ful day, O thou bless - ed day, Ho - ly,

Vir - go Ma - ri - a. Ma - ter a - ma - ta,
peace - ful Christ - mas - tide.
1. Earth's hopes a - wak - en,
2. King of glo - ry,

mp *cresc.* *mf*

in - te - me - ra - ta, O - ra, O - ra pro no - bis.
Christ life hath tak - en. Laud Him, O laud Him on ev - 'ry side.
We bow be - fore Thee,

Gaily
mf
1. Deck the halls with boughs of_ hol - ly,
2. See the blaz - ing yule be-fore us,
Fa la la la la la la la la,
mf

Deck the Halls

A legendary carol from Wales. It is one of the gayest and most beloved of the secular carols.

'Tis the sea - son to be_ jol - ly,
Strike the harp, and join the_ cho - rus,
Fa la la la la la la la la,

Don we now our gay ap-par-el,
Fol-low me in mer-ry meas-ure,
Fa la la la la la la la la,
Troll the an-cient Christ-mas car-ol,
While I tell of Christ-mas treas-ure,
Fa la la la la la la la la.

3. Fast away the old year passes,
Fa la, etc.
Hail the new! ye lads and lasses;
Fa la, etc.
Sing we joyous all together,
Fa la, etc.
Heedless of the wind and weather.
Fa la, etc.

The First Nowell

A shepherd carol of medieval days.

Gracefully

mp

1. The— first— Now-ell the— an-gel did say, Was to cer-tain poor
2. They— look - ed— up and— saw— a star Shin-ing in— the

mp

Ped. Ped. Ped. * Ped. Ped. * Ped. Ped. Ped. Ped. Ped. Ped. Ped.

shep-herds in fields as they lay; In— fields— where— they lay—
East— be - yond— them far, And— to— the— earth it—

Ped. Ped. Ped. Ped. Ped. Ped. Ped. Ped. Ped. Ped. * Ped. Ped.

keep-ing their sheep, On a cold win-ter's night that was so deep
gave great light, And so it con-tin-ued both day and night.

Now-ell, Now-ell, Now-ell, Now-ell, Born is the King of Is-ra-el.

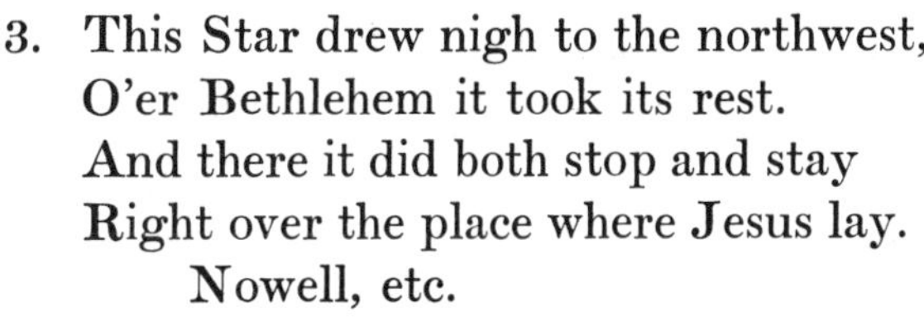

3. This Star drew nigh to the northwest,
O'er Bethlehem it took its rest.
And there it did both stop and stay
Right over the place where Jesus lay.
Nowell, etc.

4. Then enter'd in those wise men three,
Full rev'rently upon their knee,
And offer'd there in His presence,
Their gold, and myrrh, and frankincense.
Nowell, etc.

5. Then let us all with one accord
Sing praises to our heavenly Lord,
That hath made heaven and earth of nought,
And with His blood mankind hath bought.
Nowell, etc.

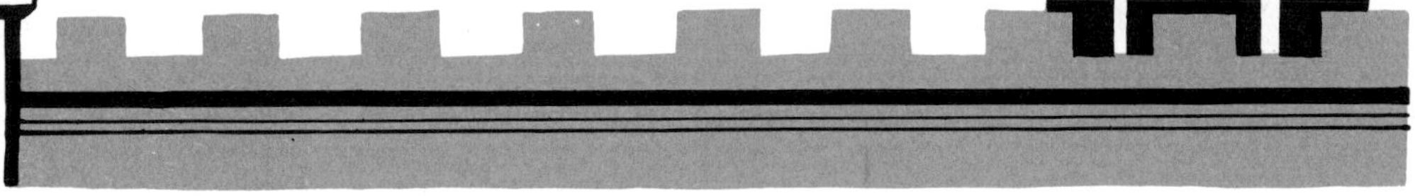

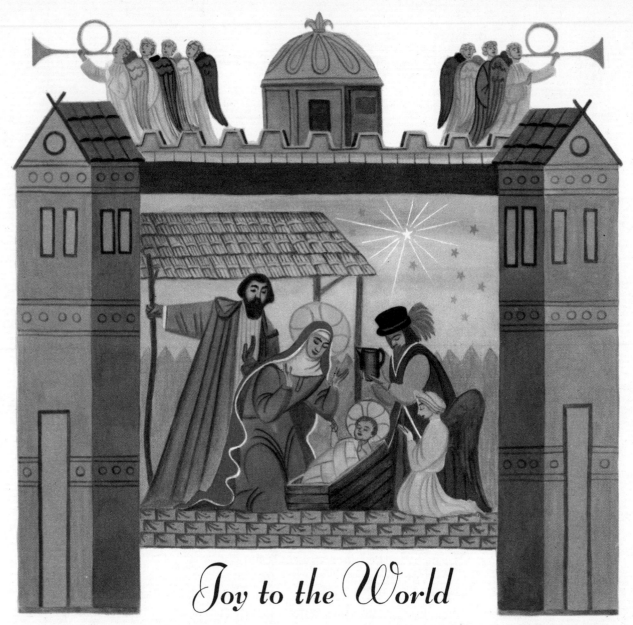

Joy to the World

A popular Christmas hymn written by Händel in 1742.

Words by Isaac Watts

Music by George F. Händel

Joyously
mf
1. Joy to the world! the Lord is come: Let earth re -
2. Joy to the world! the Sav - iour reigns; Let men their
mf

mf
ceive her King, Let ev - 'ry heart pre - pare Him
songs em - ploy, While fields and floods, rocks, hills, and
mf
room, And heav'n and na - ture sing, And heav'n and na - ture
plains Re - peat the sound - ing joy, Re - peat the sound - ing
sing, And heav'n, and heav'n and na - ture sing.
joy, Re - peat, re - peat the sound - ing joy.

3. He rules the world with truth and grace,
   And makes the nations prove
The glories of his righteousness,
The wonders of his love,
The wonders of his love,
The wonders, the wonders of his love.

God Rest You Merry, Gentlemen

An old London tune and carol.
Some versions of the song date back to the sixteenth century.

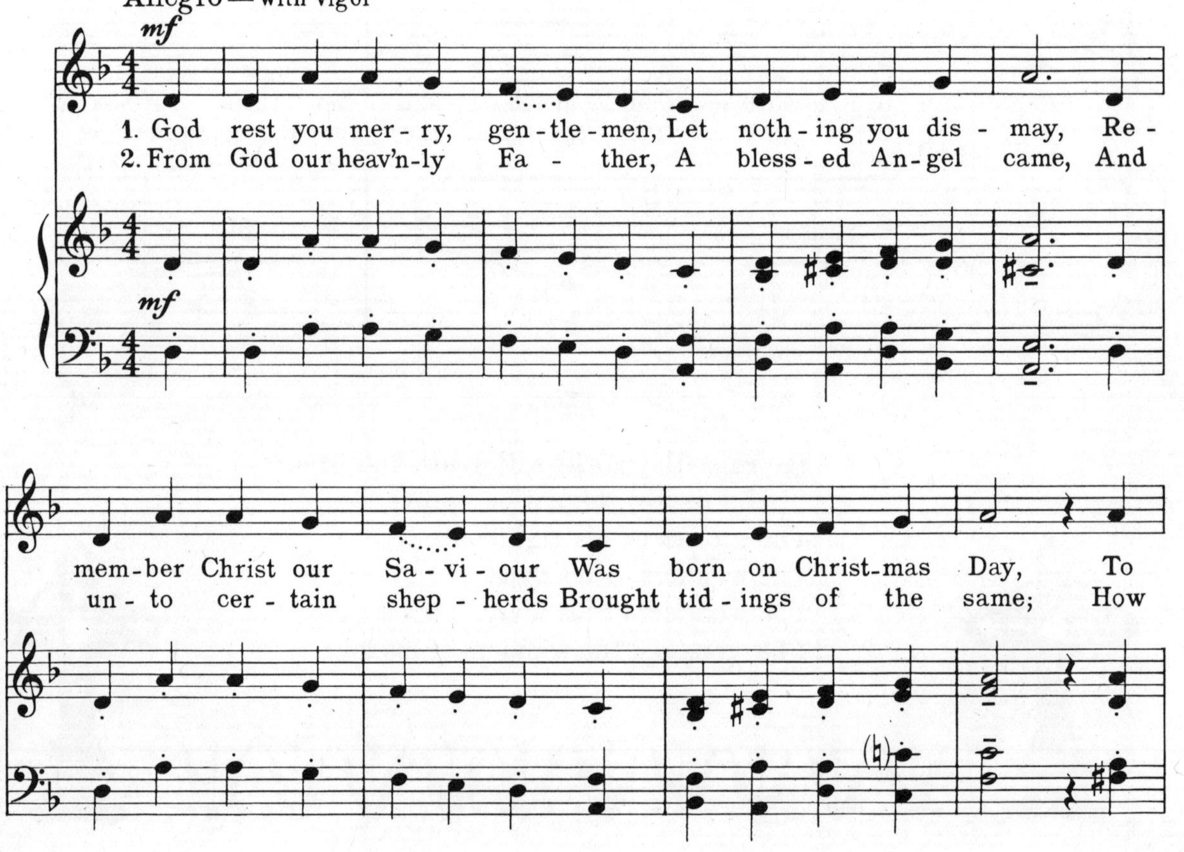
Allegro — with vigor
mf
1. God rest you mer - ry, gen - tle - men, Let noth - ing you dis - may, Re -
2. From God our heav'n-ly Fa - ther, A bless - ed An - gel came, And
mf
mem - ber Christ our Sa - vi - our Was born on Christ - mas Day, To
un - to cer - tain shep - herds Brought tid - ings of the same; How

f
save us all from Sa-tan's pow'r, When we were gone a-stray.
that in Beth-le-hem was born The Son of God by Name.
O— tid-ings of
com-fort and joy, com-fort and joy, O— tid-ings of com-fort and joy.

3.

The Shepherds at those tidings
Rejoiced much in mind
And left their flocks a-feeding
In tempest, storm, and wind,
And went straightway to Bethlehem
The Son of God to find.
O tidings, etc. . . .

4.

And when they came to Bethlehem,
Where our dear Saviour lay,
They found Him in a manger
Where oxen feed on hay;
His Mother Mary kneeling down
Unto the Lord did pray.
O tidings, etc. . . .

5.

Now to the Lord sing praises,
All you within this place,
And with true love and brotherhood
Each other now embrace;
This holy tide of Christmas
All other doth deface,
O tidings, etc. . . .

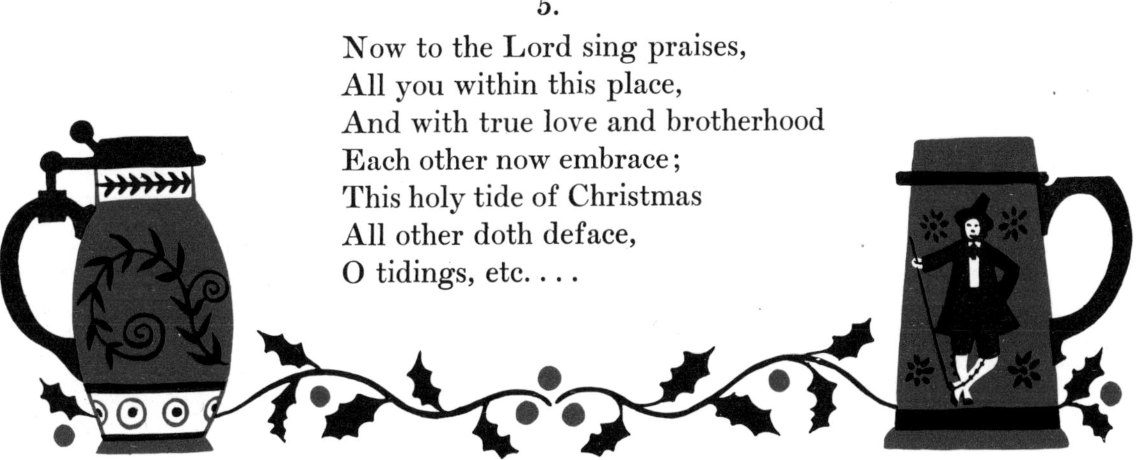

The Seven Joys of Mary

This carol was enacted in many of the mystery plays of the fifteenth century, both in England and in France.

Con moto
mf
1. The first good joy that Ma - ry had, It was the joy of
2. The next good joy that Ma - ry had, It was the joy of
mf
one;— To see the bless - ed Je - sus Christ, When He— was first— her
two;— To see her own Son Je - sus Christ— Mak-ing the lame— to

Son.— When He— was first her Son, Good Lord,
go.— Mak-ing the lame to go, Good Lord,
And hap-py may we
be;— Praise Fa-ther, Son, and Ho-ly Ghost To all e-ter-ni-ty.

3. The next good joy that Mary had,
It was the joy of three;
To see her own Son Jesus Christ
Making the blind to see.
Making the blind to see, Good Lord,
And happy, etc.

4. The next good joy that Mary had,
It was the joy of four;
To see her own Son Jesus Christ
Reading the Bible o'er.
Reading the Bible o'er, Good Lord,
And happy, etc.

5. The next good joy that Mary had,
It was the joy of five;
To see her own Son Jesus Christ
Raising the dead to life.
Raising the dead to life, Good Lord,
And happy, etc.

6. The next good joy that Mary had,
It was the joy of six;
To see her own Son Jesus Christ
Upon the Crucifix.
Upon the Crucifix, Good Lord,
And happy, etc.

7. The next good joy that Mary had,
It was the joy of seven;
To see her own Son Jesus Christ
Ascending into Heaven.
Ascending into Heaven, Good Lord,
And happy, etc.

Hark! The Herald Angels Sing

One of the best known of Mendelssohn's many beautiful Christmas songs.

Words by Charles Wesley

Music by Felix Mendelssohn-Bartholdy

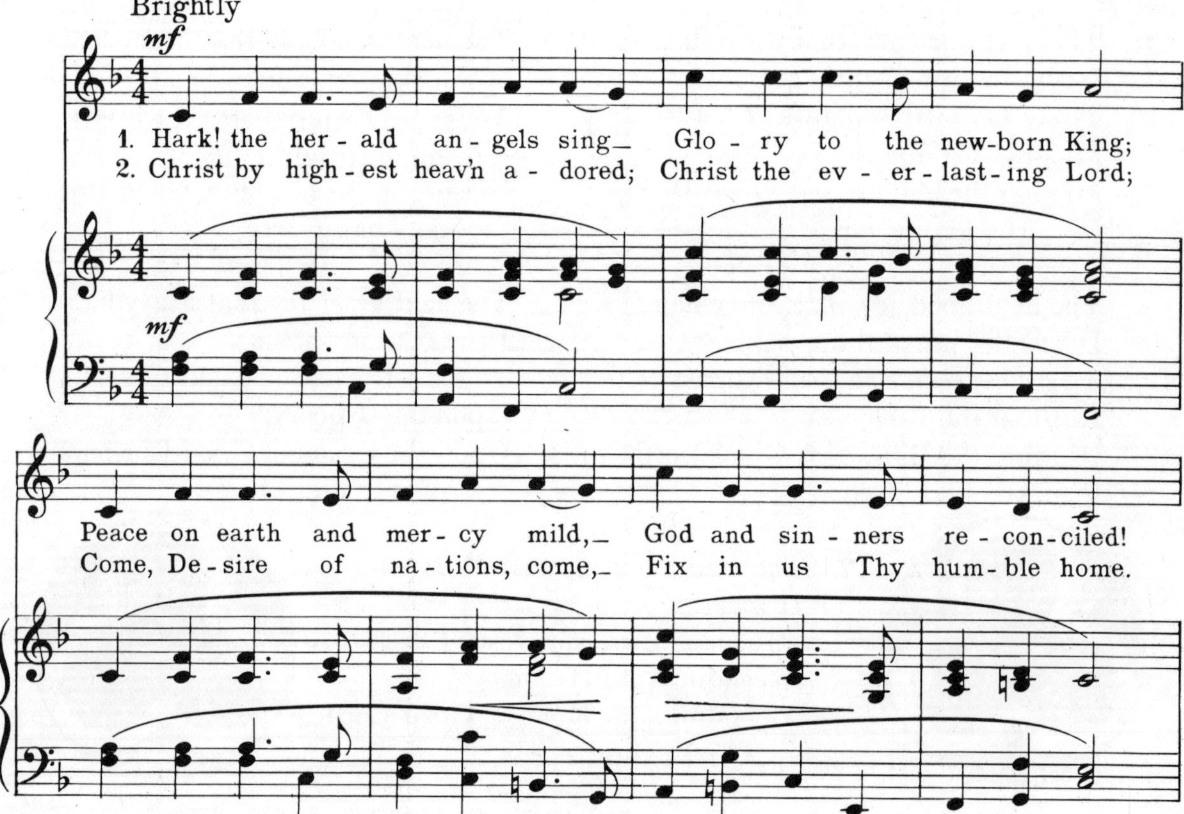
Brightly
mf
1. Hark! the her - ald an - gels sing_ Glo - ry to the new-born King;
2. Christ by high - est heav'n a - dored; Christ the ev - er - last - ing Lord;
mf
Peace on earth and mer - cy mild,_ God and sin - ners re - con - ciled!
Come, De - sire of na - tions, come,_ Fix in us Thy hum - ble home.

Joy - ful all ye na - tions rise, Join the tri - umph of the skies;
Veiled in flesh the God-head see; Hail the In - car - nate De - i - ty,
With th'an - gel - ic host pro - claim Christ is born in Beth - le - hem.
Pleased as Man with man to dwell; Je - sus our Im - man - u - el!
Hark! the her - ald an - gels sing Glo - ry to the new-born King.

3. Mild He lays His glory by,
Born that man no more may die;
Born to raise the sons of earth,
Born to give them second birth.
Ris'n with healing in His wings,
Light and life to all He brings,
Hail, the Son of Righteousness!
Hail, the heav'n-born Prince of Peace!
Hark! etc.

RISE UP, SHEPHERD, AN' FOLLER

A carol which comes to us from the Negro slaves in the United States.

Moderately fast
1. There's a star in the East on — Christ-mas morn,
2. If you take good heed to the an-gel's words,
Rise up, shep-herd, an' fol-ler;
It will lead to the place where the Sav-iour's born, —
You'll for-get yo' — flocks, you'll for-get yo' herds, —
Rise up, shep-herd, an' fol-ler!
Chorus
Fol - ler, fol - ler. Rise up, shep-herd, an' fol-ler;
Fol-ler the Star of Beth-le-hem, — Rise up, shep-herd, an' fol-ler.

Silent Night

Music by Franz Gruber

Gently
mp
1. Si - lent night, Ho - ly night! All is calm, all is bright,
2. Si - lent night, Ho - ly night! Shep-herds quake at the sight!
3. Si - lent night, Ho - ly night! Child of Heav'n, O how bright.

Round yon Vir - gin Moth-er and Child, Ho - ly In-fant so ten - der and mild;
Glo - ries stream from heav-en a - far, Heav'n-ly hosts_ sing Al - le - lu - ia;
Thou did'st smile_when Thou_wast born! Bless-ed be___ that hap - py morn,

mf
mp
Sleep in heav - en - ly peace,__ Sleep_in heav - en - ly peace.__
Christ the Sav - iour is born!__ Christ the Sav - iour is born!__
Full of heav - en - ly joy,___ Full__of heav - en - ly joy!___

Masters in This Hall
The tune is an old French carol. The words were written shortly before 1860 by William Morris.
Brightly
mf
1. Mas - ters in this Hall, Hear ye news to - day,
2. Go - ing o'er the hills; Thro' the milk-white snow,
Brought from o - ver sea, And ev - er I you pray:
Heard I ewes bleat, While the wind did blow:
f Chorus
No - well! No - well!
No - well! No-well sing we clear! Hol - pen are all folk on earth, Born

f
is God's Son so dear: No-well! No-well! No - well! No-well sing we
f

mf
loud! God to - day hath poor folk raised,_And_ cast a-down the proud.
mf

3.

Then to Bethlem town
We went two by two,
And in a sorry place
Heard the oxen low:
Chorus:

4.

Therein did we see
A sweet and goodly may
And a fair old man,
Upon the straw she lay:
Chorus:

5.

And a little child
On her arm had she.
"Wot ye who this is?"
Said the hinds to me:
Chorus:

6.

This is Christ the Lord,
Masters be ye glad!
Christmas is come in,
And no folks should be sad:
Chorus:

WASSAIL SONG

The words give a vivid picture of the English Waits, roving bands of musicians who went about the streets by night at Christmas and the New Year, playing and singing songs and carols for gratuities. The tune is from Yorkshire.

Lightly

mf

1. Here we come a - was - sail-ing, A - mong the leaves so green,__ Here we come a - wan-d'ring, So fair__ to be seen;
2. Our was - sail cup is made__ Of the rose - ma - ry tree,__ And so__ is your beer__ Of the best__ bar - ley:

mf

Ped. Ped. Ped. Ped. Ped. Ped. Ped. Ped.

Chorus

Love and joy come to you, And to you your was-sail too, And God bless you, and send__ you a

Ped. Ped. Ped. Ped. Ped. Ped. Ped. ✻ Ped. Ped.

Ped. Ped. Ped. Ped. Ped. ✻ Ped. Ped. Ped. Ped.

hap - py New Year, And God send you a hap-py New— Year.

3. We are not daily beggars
That beg from door to door,
But we are neighbors' children
Whom you have seen before.
Love and joy, etc.

4. We have got a little purse
Of stretching leather skin;
We want a little of your money
To line it well within.
Love and joy, etc.

5. Bring us out a table,
And spread it with a cloth;
Bring us out a mouldy cheese,
And some of your Christmas loaf.
Love and joy, etc.

6. God bless the master of this house,
Likewise the mistress too;
And all the little children
That round the table go.
Love and joy, etc.

OLD HYMNS AND SPIRITUALS

Old Hymns and Spirituals

FASHIONS in hymns change as in art and clothing, but the hymns for this book have been chosen for their singability and that lasting excellence which carries the best songs of every category through the centuries. The selections, ranging from the old Latin hymn "All Glory, Laud, and Honor" to the gospel hymn "Stand Up, Stand Up for Jesus," will indicate the gradual evolution of English-language hymn music.

Before the Reformation in England and in Europe, church music though excellent was entirely liturgical. The only hymns of the sort we know now were Christmas and Easter carols and a few religious songs created to be sung in the home. The customs of the Middle Ages had changed. No longer did songs, dances, and theater play a part in religious celebrations. Now, priests and monks sang in Latin, and the congregation took little part in the singing.

After the Protestant separation from the Catholic church, Luther, Huss, Calvin, and the English Reformationists developed their own ideas of church music. From this time on, songs were sung by the body of the congregation in the language spoken by the people. And although they were religious songs, they were not an integral part of the service, but a means by which the entire flock could participate in the day's lesson. Beyond this basic idea, the Protestants did not agree among themselves. Luther and Huss, drawing from the rich lore of folk hymns and carols in Germany and Bohemia, brought the music of the home to the church. If psalms were set to music in the Lutheran service they were, as in "Ein' Feste Burg," very freely translated and rendered with greater attention to their music and singability than to strict paraphrasing of the Bible. Calvin, on the other hand, sternly denounced all hymns as popish, and the music of the Calvinist church was a close, accurate metrical rendition of Bible psalms.

The Dutch and the English Protestants followed Calvin in his strict ideas of psalmody. The English Protestants who in Queen Mary's time spent their own years of exile in Switzerland brought some of Calvin's psalms back wth them when they were allowed to return to England in Elizabeth's reign. But where the Calvinists had been fortunate in having among them some excellent exile poets who wrote many of the psalms in the original French Geneva psalter, the English in their efforts to adhere to the Biblical text produced the crudest of verses.

The clumsy verses of the English Protestants were the heritage of the English-speaking American colonists in their new world. The first psalm book published in the colonies, *The Bay Psalm Book,* was taken from the English standard edition of Sternhold and Hopkins. The other book in major use was a not-much-improved book of psalms collected by a Henry Ainsworth that included some Dutch and French tunes. With their English books and the stern English ideas of church music, the American colonists were even slower than the English themselves in breaking away from them. In England, Isaac Watts not only rewrote the psalms with a freer hand, but began to turn out original hymns. John Wesley borrowed hymns from the Moravians as well as writing some of his own in the same spirit. The hymns of both men were published in America, but they did not catch on for some generations. The churches continued to cling to their ancestors' notions and stultified hymnody during a long and barren period.

In addition, the use of music in the churches, particularly in America, was actually in danger of dying out. The colonists had few and crude music instruments. There were few printers with sufficient equipment to print accompanying musical notes with the psalms. Most psalm books published the words alone, and deacons and ministers in the church had to set the tunes for the parishioners, oftening "lining out" the songs—that is, singing one line to be followed by the congregation, and then going on to the next, until the psalm was laboriously completed. The generation which came from England with the memory of psalm tunes firm in their minds died out. The new generation was so unmusical as to find even the simple tunes of the Ainsworth book difficult to sing.

Church singing was a disappearing art. It continued so until the second third of the nineteenth century. Then ministers, who had so long resisted the innovation of the new hymns from England, became the leaders of a new movement for song. They organized singing schools, brought musical instruments to the churches, and encouraged the writing of hymns by America's poets and her better musicians. The best of these took part in the movement—celebrities such as Whittier, Emerson, and Julia Ward Howe—and church music was reborn.

Along with this flowering of new and freer music, two new types of church songs grew into being. First of these was the Negro spiritual, America's greatest true folk song. For generations American slaves had sung and produced these simple, moving scriptural songs, carrying them from one plantation to another and giving birth to new and increasingly lovely versions of them. But until the Civil War the rest of the world had ignored the rich lore of their music, and its beauties had gone entirely unrecognized. The songs were recorded for the first time during the conflict between the North and South. A number of white officers of Negro regiments in the Union army wrote down the traditional melodies, and in 1867 the first collection of them, *Slave Songs of the United States,* was published. In the seventies the Jubilee Singers of Fisk University introduced the simple songs to America and to Europe, and from that time on musicians and scholars, and in particular the Negro universities of the South, have worked to search out and write down the vast stores of this purely American music.

The second type of new American hymn was the gospel song. The great religious revivals of Moody and Sankey swept the country with a wild fervor, and new hymns sprang up at the camp meetings—simple songs with catchy rhythms, sentimental words, choruses that could be echoed and re-echoed by the congregations. What wonder that such hymns aped the maudlin spirit of such contemporary popular songs as "Only a Bird in a Gilded Cage"? Hymn books flourished such titles as *Bright Jewels* and *Pure Gold.* After domination by the Puritan spirit for over a century, congregations and ministers reveled in unorthodox forms and florid words. But after the first wave of freedom, hymns became more sedate, more musical in form, better in quality.

Nineteenth-century excesses served their purpose. Restricting bugaboos were swept away. Hymns today are less denominational. Protestant hymnals are abandoning the limitations of "Methodist," "Episcopalian," "Presbyterian," or "Unitarian," and there are other freedoms of form, subject matter, and style.

The old hymns selected for this section are among the best in several centuries. But it is well to remember that even the crudest hymns of those centuries have contributed to the development of our rich body of hymn music.

A Mighty Fortress Is Our God

(EIN' FESTE BURG)

Martin Luther's original chorale, written in 1527, became the battle song of the Protestant warriors. It was translated in 1853 by Frederic Henry Hedge. In 1942 once again it served as a battle hymn and was sung by the free Norwegians in defiance of a Nazi order to close the ancient Trondheim Cathedral.

Translation by E. H. Hedge

Music by Martin Luther

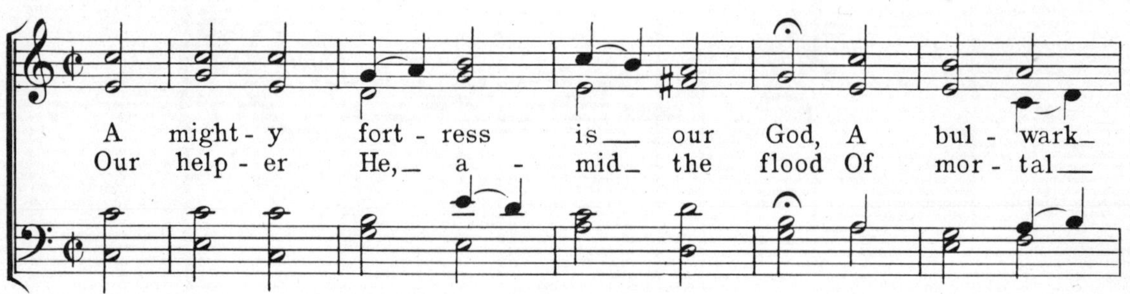
A might - y fort - ress is_ our God, A bul - wark_
Our help - er He,_ a - mid_ the flood Of mor - tal_

nev - er— fail - - ing; For still our an - cient foe Doth
ills— pre - vail - - ing.

seek to work us woe; His craft and pow'r are— great, And

arm'd with— cru - el hate, On earth— is not his— e - - qual.

2. Did we in our own strength confide,
Our striving would be losing;
Were not the right man on our side,
The man of God's own choosing.
Dost ask who that may be?
Christ Jesus, it is He;
Lord Sabaoth His Name,
From age to age the same,
And He must win the battle.

3. And though this world, with devils filled,
Should threaten to undo us;
We will not fear, for God hath willed
His truth to triumph through us:
The prince of darkness grim,—
We tremble not for him;
His rage we can endure,
For lo! his doom is sure,
One little word shall fell him.

4. That word above all earthly pow'rs,
No thanks to them, abideth;
The Spirit and the gifts are ours
Through Him who with us sideth:
Let goods and kindred go,
This mortal life also;
The body they may kill:
God's truth abideth still,
His kingdom is forever.

Who Can Retell?

A Palestinian folk song.

Allegro
mf
Who can re-tell the things that be-fell us? Who can count them?
mf
Fine
In ev-'ry age a he-ro or sage Came to our aid. Ah!
Fine
Ped. Ped.

At this time of year in days of yore
Mac-ca-bees the Tem-ple did re-
store,
And to-day our peo-ple, as we dreamed,
will a-rise, u-nite, and be re-deemed.
D.C. al Fine
D.C. al Fine

My Faith Looks Up to Thee

(OLIVET)

This is one of the important hymns in the collection Spiritual Songs, *published by Lowell Mason and Thomas Hastings in 1832. The words were written by a friend of Mason's, Ray Palmer, in 1830, and were set by Mason to his own tune, "Olivet."*

Words by Ray Palmer

Music by Lowell Mason

1. My faith looks up to Thee, Thou Lamb of Cal-va-ry, Sav-iour di-
2. May Thy rich grace im-part Strength to my faint-ing heart, My zeal in-
vine! Now hear me while I pray, Take all my guilt a-way, O let me
spire; As Thou hast died for me, O— may my love to Thee Pure, warm, and
from this day Be whol-ly Thine.
change-less be, A liv-ing fire.

3. While life's dark maze I tread,
And griefs around me spread,
Be Thou my guide;
Bid darkness turn to day,
Wipe sorrow's tears away,
Nor let me ever stray
From Thee aside.

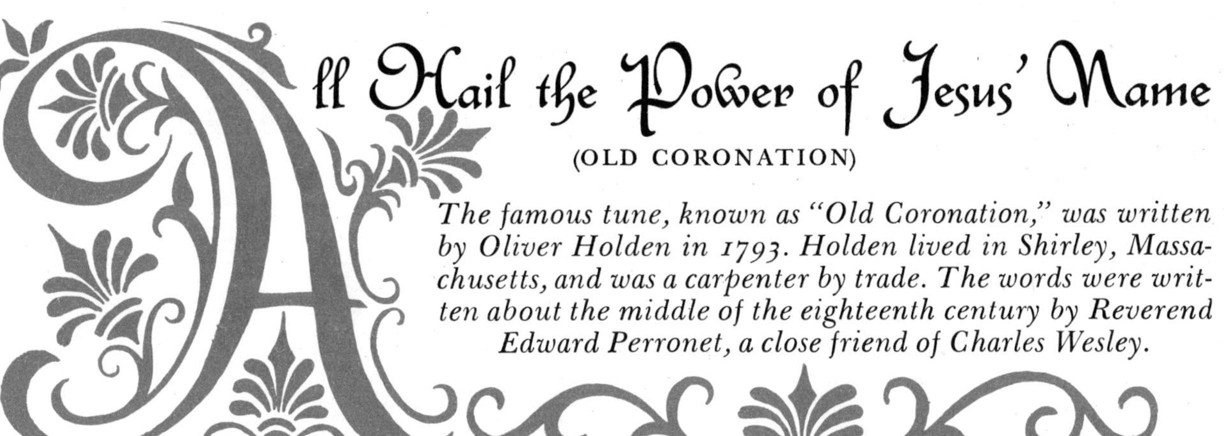

All Hail the Power of Jesus' Name

(OLD CORONATION)

The famous tune, known as "Old Coronation," was written by Oliver Holden in 1793. Holden lived in Shirley, Massachusetts, and was a carpenter by trade. The words were written about the middle of the eighteenth century by Reverend Edward Perronet, a close friend of Charles Wesley.

Words by Rev. Edward Perronet — Music by Oliver Holden

1. All hail the pow'r of Je - sus' name, Let an - gels pros-trate fall; Bring
2. Crown Him, ye mar - tyrs of our God, Who from His al - tar call; Ex -

forth the roy - al di - a - dem, And crown Him Lord of all! Bring
tol the Stem of Jes - se's Rod, And crown Him Lord of all! Ex -

forth the roy - al di - a - dem, And crown Him Lord of all!
tol the Stem of Jes - se's Rod, And crown Him Lord of all!

3. Ye seed of Israel's chosen race,
Ye ransomed of the fall,
Hail Him Who saves you by His grace,
And crown Him Lord of all!
Hail Him, etc.

4. Let every kindred, every tribe,
Before Him prostrate fall.
To Him all majesty ascribe,
And crown Him Lord of all!
To Him, etc.

Glee Reigns in Galilee

Gilu Hagalilim, a song of Zion, was probably written within the last twenty years. It has the strong rhythm of the dance and should be sung joyously.

Translation by A. N. Dushkin

Allegro
mf
1. Glee reigns in Ga - li - lee, The Ga - lil re - joic - es;
mf

English words by A. M. Dushkin.

Fine
mp
The day and night—'round—Lift up your voic - es.
2.Thru night's—
3. Sing ho, my
mp
witch-ing dark-ness, Flutes soft - ly sound - ing, The watch-man of Ga - li - lee. His
Ga - li - lee, O, sing on my heart - strings;— With gun and no-ble steed, I
watch-song re - sound - ing.
fear not what fate brings.
D. C.
D. C.

4. Who am I, what have I
Without thee, my Galil?
Glorious Galilee,
I love thee, my Galil.
Glee reigns, etc.

Guide Me, O Thou Great Jehovah
The words were written by William Williams, famed as the "sweet singer of Wales." It was translated from the Welsh by the Reverend Peter Williams in 1771. The original music for the hymn was written by Thomas Olivers.
Translation by Peter Williams
Music by François H. Barthélémon
1. Guide me, O Thou great Je - ho - vah, Pil - grim through this bar - ren
2. Feed me with the heav'n-ly man - na In this bar - ren wil - der -
land, I am weak, but Thou art might - y; Hold me with Thy pow'r - ful
ness; Be my sword, and shield, and ban - ner, Be the Lord my Right - eous -
hand. O - pen now the crys - tal foun - tains Whence the liv - ing wa - ters
ness. When I tread the verge of Jor - dan, Bid my anx - ious fears sub -
flow; Let the fier - y cloud - y pil - lar Lead me all my jour - ney through.
side; Death of death, and hell's de - struc - tion, Land me safe on Ca - naan's side.

OLD HUNDREDTH

The tune is first found in the French Genevan Psalter of 1551. It was sung by our forefathers in this early form, in fairly quick time, and was thought by them to be "a jocund and lively air." It emerged from the eighteenth century a solemn and stately tune, its gay character entirely lost.

Words by Thomas Ken

Music by Louis Bourgeois

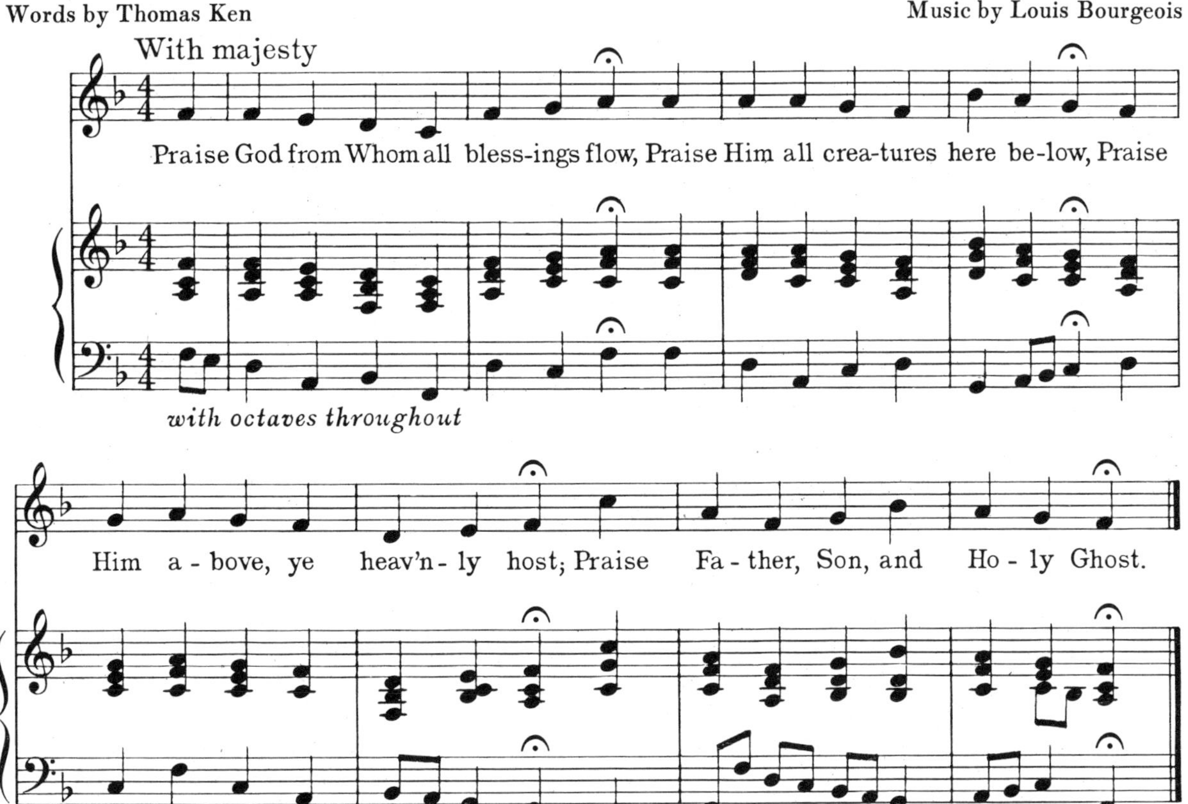
With majesty
Praise God from Whom all bless-ings flow, Praise Him all crea-tures here be-low, Praise
with octaves throughout
Him a - bove, ye heav'n - ly host; Praise Fa - ther, Son, and Ho - ly Ghost.

Day Is Dying in the West

This most widely used hymn of American origin was written by the famous Methodist hymn writer, Mary Artemesia Lathbury, for use at Chautauqua in 1877.

Words by Mary A. Lathbury — Music by William F. Sherwin

1. Day is dy - ing in the west, Heav'n is touch - ing earth with rest; Wait and wor - ship while the night Sets her eve - ning lamps a - light, Thro' all the sky.

2. Lord of life, be - neath the dome Of the u - ni - verse, Thy home, Gath - er us who seek Thy face To the fold of Thy em - brace, For Thou art nigh.

Refrain

Ho - ly, Ho - ly, Ho - ly, Lord God of Hosts! Heav'n and earth are full of Thee, Heav'n and earth are prais - ing Thee, O Lord most High!

3. When forever from our sight
Pass the stars, the day, the night,
Lord of angels, on our eyes
Let eternal morning rise,
And shadows end.
Holy, etc.

Fairest Lord Jesus

(CRUSADER'S HYMN)

The words are a translation of an anonymous seventeenth-century German hymn. The tune is said to be a Silesian melody, first published in Leipzig in 1842.

1. Fair - est Lord Je - sus, Rul - er of all na - ture,
2. Fair are the mead - ows, Fair - er still the wood - lands

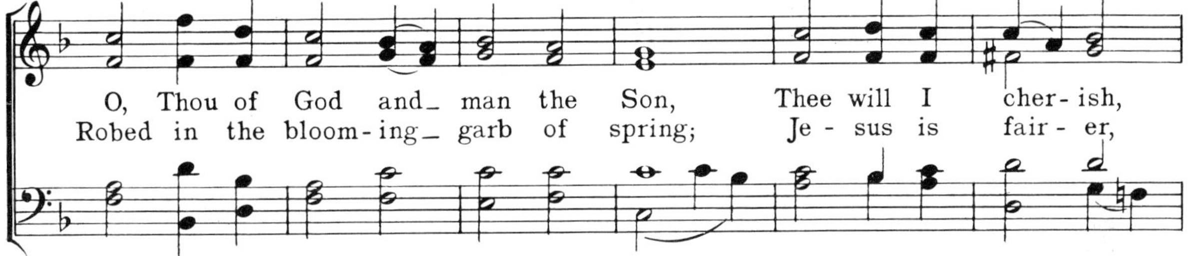
O, Thou of God and_ man the Son, Thee will I cher - ish,
Robed in the bloom - ing_ garb of spring; Je - sus is fair - er,

Thee will I hon - or, Thou, my soul's glo - ry, joy and_ crown.
Je - sus is pur - er, Who makes the woe - ful heart to_ sing.

3. Fair is the sunshine,
Fairer still the moonlight,
And all the twinkling, starry host;
Jesus shines brighter, Jesus shines purer
Than all the angels heav'n can boast.

Stand Up, Stand Up, for Jesus

A gospel hymn written during the great revival of 1859. Its stirring, militant quality made it a favorite with the soldiers of the Union army during the Civil War.

Words by George Duffield

Music by George J. Webb

1. Stand up, stand up for Je - sus, Ye sol-diers of the Cross, Lift
2. Stand up, stand up for Je - sus, The trum-pet call o - bey, Forth

high His roy - al ban - ner, It must not suf - fer loss. From vic - t'ry un - to
to the might - y con - flict, In this His glo-rious day. Ye that are men now

vic - t'ry His ar - my shall He lead, _ Till ev - 'ry foe is van-quished, And
serve Him A - gainst un-num-bered foes: _ Let cour - age rise with dan - ger, And

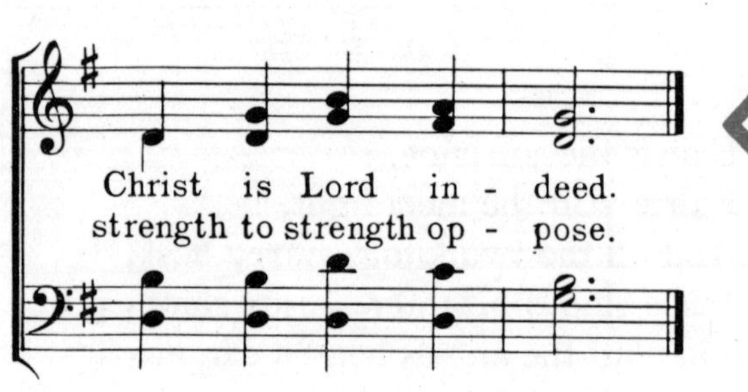
Christ is Lord in - deed.
strength to strength op - pose.

3. Stand up, stand up for Jesus,
The strife will not be long;
This day, the noise of battle,
The next, the victor's song.
To him that overcometh
A crown of life shall be;
He with the King of Glory
Shall reign eternally.

Jesus, Saviour, Pilot Me

A sailors' hymn of the gospel-song period. The poem, by Reverend Edward Hopper, was published anonymously in The Sailors' Magazine *in 1871.*

Words by Rev. Edward Hopper

Music by J. E. Gould

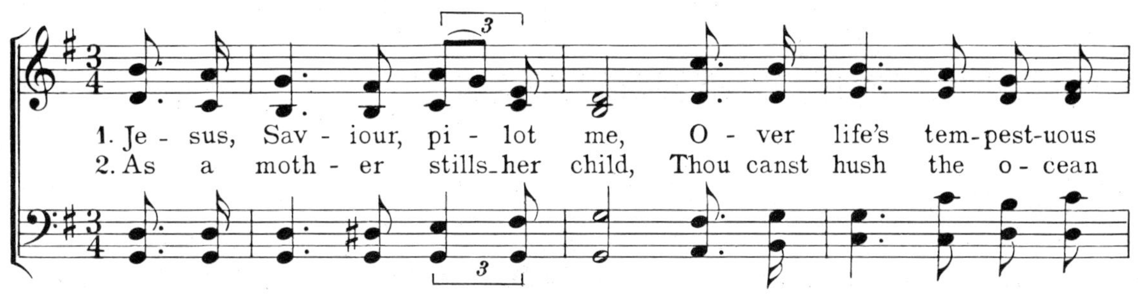
3
1. Je - sus, Sav - iour, pi - lot me, O - ver life's tem-pest-uous
2. As a moth - er stills_her child, Thou canst hush the o - cean
3

sea; Un - known waves be - fore me roll, Hid - ing rock and treach-'rous
wild; Bois - t'rous waves o - bey Thy will When Thou say'st to them, "Be

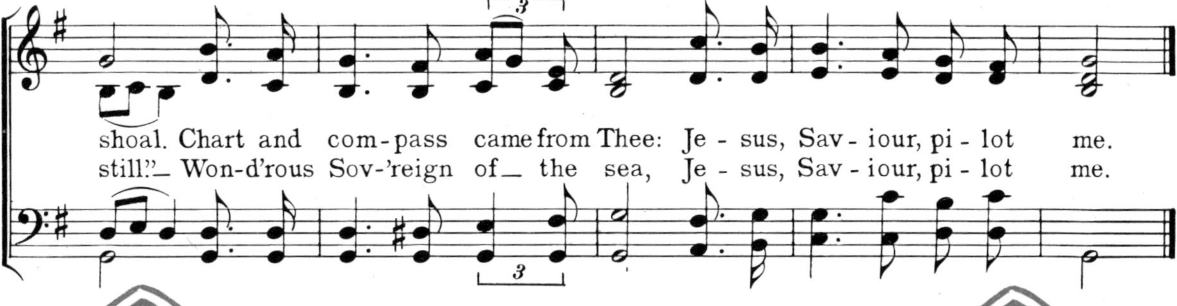
3
shoal. Chart and com-pass came from Thee: Je - sus, Sav - iour, pi - lot me.
still!"_ Won-d'rous Sov-'reign of_ the sea, Je - sus, Sav - iour, pi - lot me.
3

3. When at last I near the shore,
And the fearful breakers roar
'Twixt me and the peaceful rest;
Then, while leaning on Thy breast,
May I hear Thee say to me,
"Fear not, I will pilot thee."

אור
Hanukkah Song
The Hebrew Hanukkah, or Festival of Lights, was first celebrated in November, 165 B.C. The festival continues for eight days, and a candle is lit for each day. A special candle, called the Shamos, is used for lighting the others. The words here are sung to an old Yiddish folk song.
Allegro
mf
O Ha-nuk-kah, O Ha-nuk-kah, come light the me-no-rah! Let's have a par-ty, we'll
all dance the ho-rah. Gath-er 'round the ta-ble, we'll give you a treat,

S'vi-vo-nim to play with, le - vi - vot to eat. And while we are
play-ing, The can-dles are burn-ing_ low. One for each night, They_
shed a sweet light, To re-mind us of days long a - go.
One for each night, They shed a sweet light, To re-mind us of days long a - go.

All Glory, Laud, and Honor

A stately hymn of the ninth century. It was composed in 820 A.D. by St. Theodulph, Bishop of Orleans, while a captive in the cloister of Anjou. The melody, by Melchior Teschner, was written in 1619.

Translation by John Mason Neale | **Music by Melchior Teschner**

1. All glo - ry, laud, and hon - or To Thee, Re - deem - er, King! To
whom the lips of chil - dren Made sweet ho - san - nas ring. *Fine*

2. Thou art the King of Is - ra - el, Thou Da - vid's roy - al Son, Who
in the Lord's name com - eth, The King and Bless - ed One. *D. C.*

3. The peo - ple of the He - brews With palms be - fore Thee went; Our
praise and prayers and an - thems Be - fore Thee we pre - sent.

4. To Thee before Thy Passion
They sang their hymns of praise;
To Thee, now high exalted,
Our melody we raise.
All glory, etc.

5. Thou didst accept their praises,
Accept the pray'rs we bring,
Who in all good delighteth,
Thou good and gracious King.
All glory, etc.

Who Is the Man?

One of the hymns in the Ainsworth Psalter, which the Pilgrim Fathers used in Holland and which they brought with them to America. The melody is an ancient folk song. It was used by Martin Luther in his chorale of the Lord's Prayer (1539), and later by J. S. Bach in his St. John's Passion

With firmness
mf
* See below
1. Who is the man, that life doth will; That lov-eth dayes, good for to see?
2. In all time bless the Lord will I, His praise with-in my mouth, al-way.
mf
with pedal
Re-freyn-ing, keep thy tongue from yll, Thy lips from speak-ing fal-la-cee.
My soul shall in the Lord glo-ry; The meek shall heare, and joy shall they.
Doo good, and e-vil quite es-chew, Seek peace and af-ter it pur-sew.
O mag-ni-fie the Lord with me, His name to-geth-er ex-toll we.

* NOTE: This hymn must be sung in complete phrases of seven counts plus the "hold," which adds another count for taking a breath.

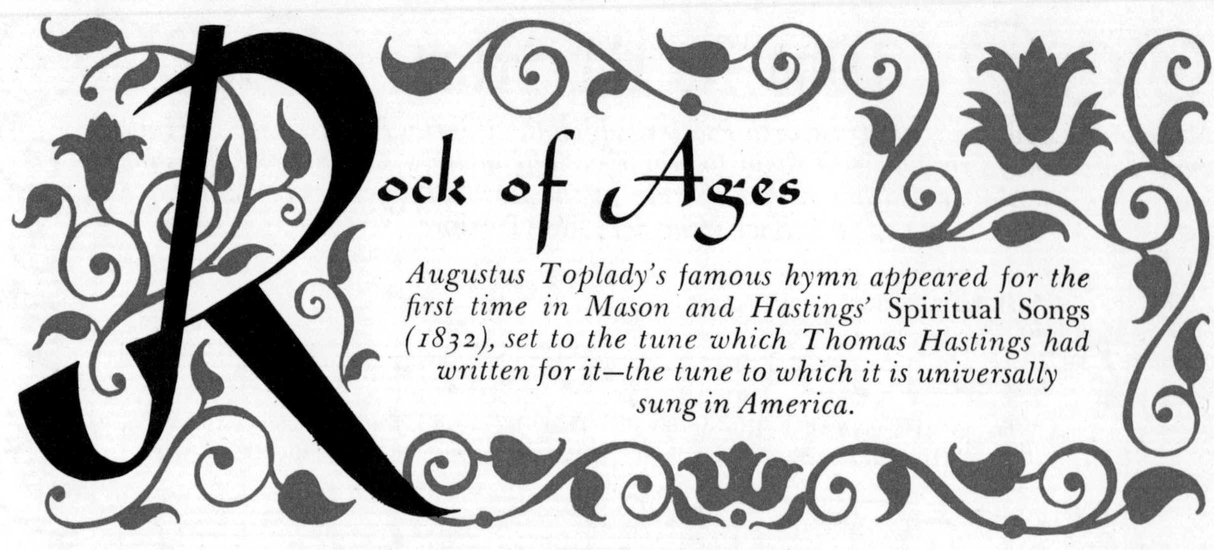
Rock of Ages
Augustus Toplady's famous hymn appeared for the first time in Mason and Hastings' Spiritual Songs (1832), set to the tune which Thomas Hastings had written for it—the tune to which it is universally sung in America.

Words by Augustus M. Toplady
Music by Thomas Hastings
1. Rock of a - ges, cleft for me, Let me hide my- self in
2. Should my tears for - ev - er flow, Should my zeal no lan-guor
Thee; Let the wa - ter and the blood, From Thy side, a heal- ing
know, All for sin could not a - tone, Thou must save, and Thou a -
flood, Be of sin the dou - ble cure, Save from wrath, and make me pure.
lone; In my hand no price I bring, Sim-ply to Thy cross I cling.

3. While I draw this fleeting breath,
When mine eyelids close in death,
When I rise to worlds unknown,
And behold Thee on Thy throne,
Rock of ages, cleft for me,
Let me hide myself in Thee.

Shall We Gather at the River

In the nineteenth century a revival movement under Dwight E. Moody and Ira G. Sankey swept over the United States. The gospel songs which resulted were of a new type, an answer to "a search for an utterance more to the popular liking." This Methodist hymn was one of the most famous of the period.

Words and Music by Rev. Robert Lowry

Con moto
1. Shall we gath- er at the riv - er Where bright an- gel feet have trod; —
2. Ere we reach the shin-ing riv - er Lay we ev- 'ry bur- den down; —
With its crys- tal tide for- ev - er Flow-ing by the throne of — God?
Grace our spir- its will de - liv - er, And pro - vide a — robe and — crown.
Chorus
Yes, we'll gath- er at the riv - er, The beau- ti- ful, the beau- ti- ful — riv - er;
Gath- er with the saints at the riv - er, That flows by the throne of — God.

3. Soon we'll reach the silver river,
Soon our pilgrimage will cease,
Soon our happy hearts will quiver
With the melody of peace.
Yes, we'll gather, etc.

STEAL AWAY

A NOTE ABOUT SPIRITUALS

These religious folk songs grew out of the miseries of slavery and were sung long before the Proclamation of Emancipation. No one knows their exact origin, for they were carried by slaves from plantation to plantation, from state to state. Said Booker T. Washington: "No race has ever sung so sweetly, or with such perfect charity, while looking forward to the 'year of Jubilo.'"

p Chorus
mp
Steal a - way, steal a - way, Steal a - way to Je - sus;
legato
p

p
p subito
Fine
Steal a-way, steal_ a-way home, I ain't got long to stay here.
p subito
f
1. My Lord__ calls me; He calls me by the thun-der,
2. Green trees a-bend-in'; Poor sin-ner stands a-tremb-lin',
The
trum-pet sounds with-in-a my soul, I ain't got long to stay here.
D. C.
Ped. Ped.

NOW LET ME FLY

Con moto

mf

1. Way down yon-der in de mid-dle o' de fiel', An-gel work-in' at de char-iot wheel, Not so par-tic-'lar 'bout
2. I got a moth-er in de Pro-mise Lan', Ain't goin' to stop till I shake her han', Not so par-tic-'lar 'bout
3. Meet dat Hy-po-crite on de street, First thing he do is to show his teeth. Nex' thing he do is to

mf

work-in' at de wheel, But I jes' want-a see— how de char-iot feel.
shak-in' her— han', But I jes' want-a get up in de Pro-mise Lan'.
tell— a— lie, An' de bes' thing to do— is to pass him by.
Chorus
Now let me fly,— Now let me fly,— Now
let me fly— in-to Mount Zi-on, Lord, Lord.—
Ped.
Ped.
Ped.
Ped.

NOBODY KNOWS DE TROUBLE I SEE

Slowly, but with motion
mp Chorus
No-bod-y knows de trou-ble I see, No-bod-y knows but Je - sus;
mp
Ped. Ped. Ped. Ped. Ped. Ped. Ped. Ped.

1 2 Fine
No-bod-y knows de trou-ble I see, Glo - ry hal-le - lu - jah! Oh, lu - jah!
hurry , slower ,
1. Some - times I'm up, some - times I'm down, Oh, yes, Lord; Some-
2. Al - tho' you see me goin' 'long so, Oh, yes, Lord; I
hurry slower
1 2 D.C.
times I'm al-most to de groun', Oh, yes, Lord.
have my tri-als here be-low, Oh, yes, Lord. Oh,
D.C.

JOSHUA FIT DE BATTLE OB JERICO

Not too fast

mf *Chorus*

Josh-ua fit de bat-tle ob Jer-i-co, Jer-i-co,

Jer-i-co, Josh-ua fit de bat-tle ob

Jer-i-co, An' de walls come tum-bel-in' down.

Fine

1. You kin talk a - bout yo' king ob Gid - e - on, You kin talk a - bout yo' man ob Saul, But dere's none like good ole Josh - ua. At de bat - tle ob Jer - i - co Dat morn - in'
2. Up to de walls ob Jer - i - co, Dey marched wid spear in han'. Go blow dem ram horns, Josh - ua cried, 'Case de bat - tle am in my han' Dat morn - in'
D.C.

3. Den de lam'-ram sheep-horns begin to blow,
De trumpets begin to soun',
Ole Joshua commanded de chillen to shout—
An' de walls come tumblin' down, dat mornin'
Chorus:

Oh, a-Rock-a My Soul

Fast
mf
Oh, a - rock - a my soul, In de bo - som of A - bra - ham, A -
mf
Ped. Ped. Ped. Ped.

rock-a my soul, In de bo-som of A - bra-ham, A - rock-a my soul, In de
bo - som of A - bra - ham, Oh, rock - a my soul.
Fine
Slower
p Solo
1. When I went down in the val-ley to pray,
2. When I was a mourn-er jes' like you,
mf Chorus
Oh, rock-a my soul,
p Solo
My
I
soul got hap-py an' I stay'd all day,
mourned and mourned 'til I come through,
mf Chorus
Oh, rock-a my soul.
D. C.

ONE MORE RIVER

Rollicking
mf Solo
Chorus
1. Old No - ah once he built the Ark,
2. He went to work to load his stock,
There's one more riv - er to
mf
Solo
Chorus
cross.
And patched_ it up with hick-o - ry bark,
He an-chored the Ark with a great_ big rock,
There's one more riv - er to
mf
f Chorus
cross. One more riv - er,___ and that's the riv - er of Jor - dan,
f

One more riv - er, There's one more riv - er to cross. 2. He

3. The animals went in one by one,
The elephant chewing a caraway bun,
Chorus:

4. The animals went in two by two,
The rhinoceros and the kangaroo,
Chorus:

5. The animals went in three by three,
The bear, the flea and the bumble bee,
Chorus:

6. The animals went in four by four,
Old Noah got mad and hollered for more,
Chorus:

7. The animals went in five by five,
With Saratoga trunks they did arrive,
Chorus:

8. The animals went in six by six,
The hyena laughed at the monkey's tricks,
Chorus:

9. The animals went in seven by seven,
Said the ant to the elephant, who are you a-shovin'?
Chorus:

10. The animals went in eight by eight,
They came with a rush 'cause 'twas so late,
Chorus:

11. The animals went in nine by nine,
Old Noah shouted, "Cut that line!"—
Chorus:

12. The animals went in ten by ten,
The Ark she blew her whistle then,
Chorus:

13. And then the voyage did begin,
Old Noah pulled the gang-plank in,
Chorus:

14. They never knew where they were at,
Till the old Ark bumped on Ararat,
Chorus:

CHORUS

One more river,—and that's the river of Jordan,
One more river,
There's one more river to cross.

Swing Low, Sweet Chariot

Slowly, with elation

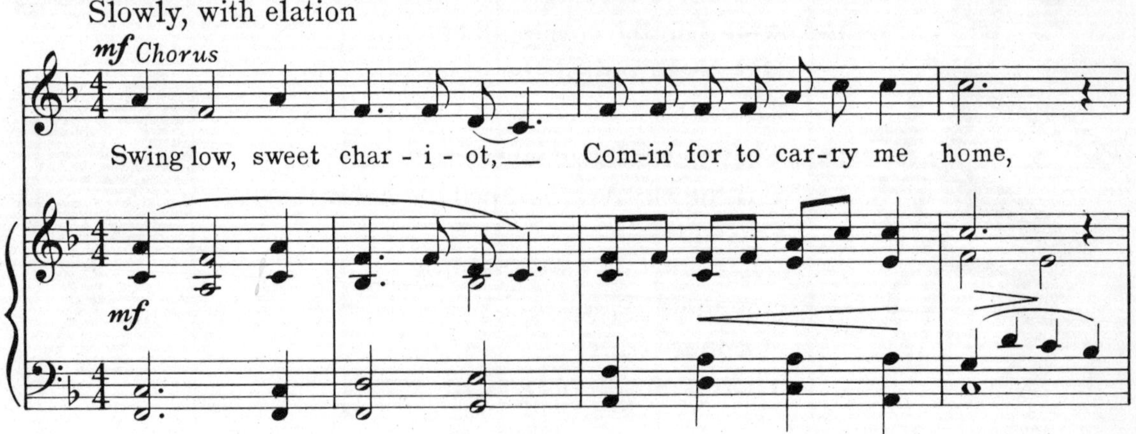
mf Chorus
Swing low, sweet char - i - ot,
Com-in' for to car-ry me home,
mf

poco rit.
a tempo
Fine
Swing low, sweet char - i - ot, Com-in' for to car-ry me home.
a tempo
Fine
poco rit.
Solo
poco rit.
1. I look'd o - ver Jor-dan an' what did I see,
2. If you get there be - fore I do,
poco rit.
Chorus
a tempo
Solo
Com-in' for to car-ry me home,
A band of an - gels
Tell all my friends I'm
a tempo
p
poco rit.
Chorus
Resolutely
D.C.
com-in' af - ter me,
com-in' there too,
Com-in' for to car-ry me home. O
poco rit.
Resolutely
D.C.
mf

Sit Down, Sister

With happiness

mf *Chorus*

Oh, won't you sit down? — Lawd, I can't sit down, — Oh, won't you sit down? — Lawd, I can't sit down, — Oh, won't you sit down? — Lawd, I can't sit down, 'Cause I just got to Heav-en, Goin' to look a - round. —

Fine

mf

Fine

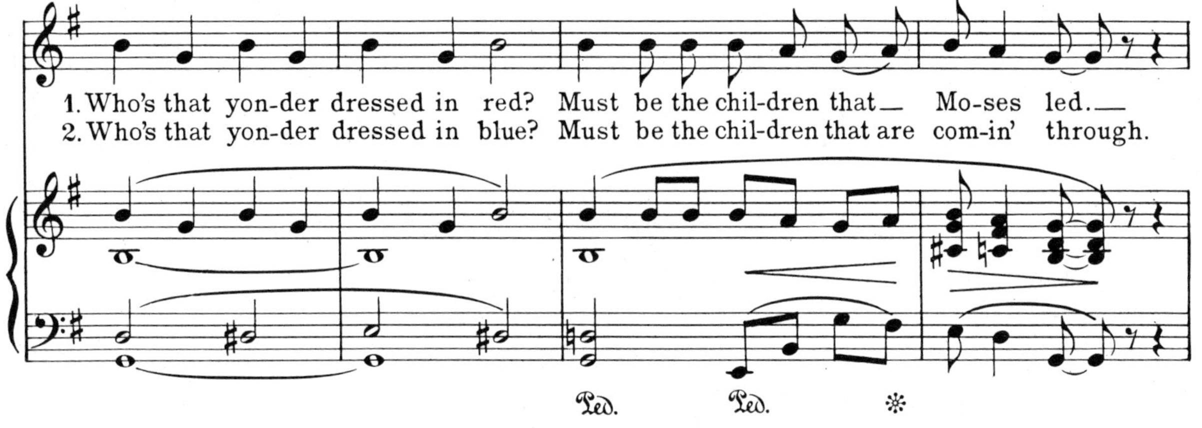
1. Who's that yon-der dressed in red? Must be the chil-dren that__ Mo-ses led.__
2. Who's that yon-der dressed in blue? Must be the chil-dren that are com-in' through.
Ped. Ped. *

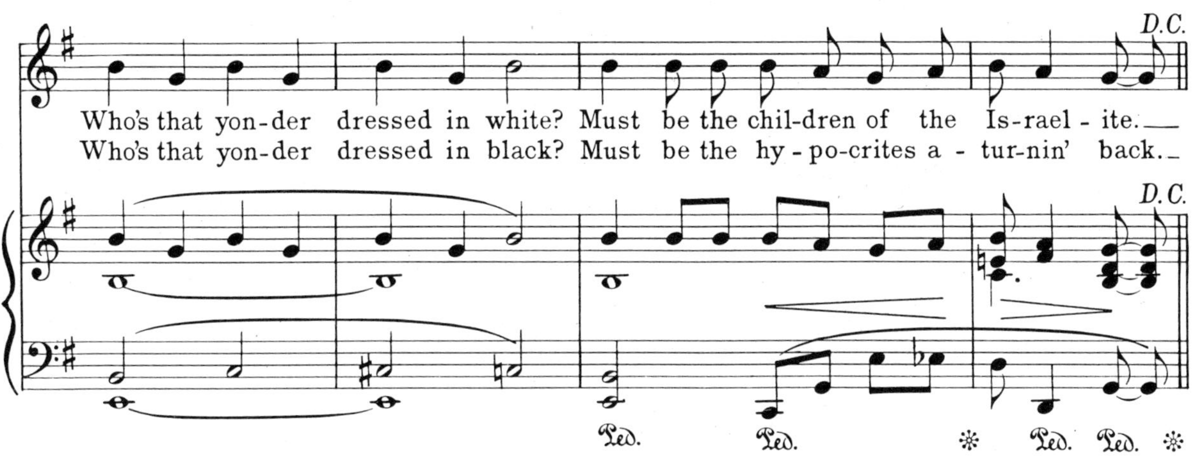
D.C.
Who's that yon-der dressed in white? Must be the chil-dren of the Is-rael - ite.__
Who's that yon-der dressed in black? Must be the hy - po-crites a - tur-nin' back.__
D.C.
Ped. Ped. * Ped. Ped. *

My Lord, What a Morning

With ecstacy
mf Chorus
My Lord, what a morn-ing, My Lord, what a morn-ing,

Fine
My Lord, what a morn-ing, When the stars be-gin to fall.
Fine
1. You'll hear the trum-pet sound
2. You'll hear the sin-ners mourn
3. You'll hear the Chris-tians shout
To wake the na-tions un-der-ground,
f
D.C.
Look-ing to my God's right hand, When the stars be-gin to fall.
D.C.

GO DOWN, MOSES
Boldly
mf
1. When Is-rael was in E-gyp' Lan',
2. Thus spoke the Lord, bold Mo-ses said,
Let my peo-ple go, Op-
If
pressed so hard they could not stan',
not I'll smite your first-born dead,
Let my peo-ple go.
f Chorus
Go down, Mo-ses,
Way down in E-gyp' Lan', Tell ol' Pha-raoh To let my peo-ple go.
poco rit.
a tempo

Index of First Lines

Index of Titles

ABOUT THE CONTRIBUTORS

THE EDITOR: *Margaret Bradford Boni* says of herself:

"I was born in Birmingham, Alabama, and lived in Tallahassee, Florida, from the age of one until I finished college—Florida State College. Studied music in Germany for a year, then studied at the Institute of Musical Art (now the Juilliard School of Music). Decided to go into school music and worked with Hollis Dann, state supervisor of music in Pennsylvania, for my supervisor's degree.

"My first job was in a small town in Pennsylvania, Factoryville by name. I taught music in the public schools there—grammar and high school. In the high school I had some pretty big, tough boys who had never done much singing. After a brief period of hostility we struck an agreement with each other: if I would coach them in basketball, they would come to my chorus and sing. It worked splendidly, and when we got really to trust each other they generously threw in one more thing: they taught me to skate.

"My next job was at the Brearley School, New York City (quite a change!). After five or six years there I came to City and Country School, where I now am.

"In each of these schools—so different in every way from one another—I found that folk-song literature was the answer to the needs and interests of the children: work songs, labor songs, songs of the people of America and other countries—these they would sing and enjoy and want more of. And so my own interest grew, and I have for years made collections of folk songs and sung them with grown-ups and children.

"I also studied ancient instruments with Arnold Dolmetsch in England, through him became interested in the recorders, brought them back to America with me, and introduced them in the schools here and to various groups of adults. Have written six books of recorder material and have published a collection of songs for very young children, KEEP SINGING, KEEP HUMMING. Have also given recorder courses in the Department of General Education, New York University."

THE ARRANGER: *Norman Lloyd,* who is Director of Education at the Juilliard School of Music in New York City, has had a widely varied career in music. Seven years after his birth in Pottsville, Pennsylvania, in 1909, he was studying piano and theory at the Braun School of Music. He has received the B.S. and M.A. degrees in Music Education from New York University, studied piano with Abbey Whiteside and William O'Toole, and explored composition with Vincent Jones and Aaron Copland. As music director of the Bennington School of Dance and of the Humphrey-Weidman Dance Company, and Conductor of the Sarah Lawrence College Chorus, he became a seasoned conductor. He has taught music at New York University, Sarah Lawrence College, the Humphrey-Weidman Dance Studio, and the Hanya Holm School of Dance, and, finally, in his present capacity at the Juilliard School. Among his own musical creations are a number of compositions for documentary films produced by the Office of War Information and the Coordinator of Inter-American Affairs, besides miscellaneous works including songs, choral works, sonatas, and pieces for the piano.

THE ARTISTS: The biographies of *Alice and Martin Provensen* are practically the same. They were born in the same city—Chicago; they won scholarships at and attended the same art school—The Chicago Art Institute; they attended the same university—The University of California; and they have both worked in Hollywood in the production of animated-cartoon films—Alice in the animation department of Universal and Martin at the Disney Studio, where he helped in the creation of such films as "Dumbo," "Fantasia," "Pinocchio," and "Peter and the Wolf." They did not finally meet, however, until Martin had joined the Navy and was assigned to Navy training film work at the same studio where Alice was working. They then immediately decided to join forces and collaborate in earnest for the rest of their lives. The Provensens are now living in New York City and concentrating on book illustration.